3DS MAX

2019 TRAINING GUIDE

By

Linkan Sagar
Nisha Gupta

Illegal for sale
or distribution outside
Indian Sub-continent.
Books found outside this
market may be treated as
illegal/ pirated books.

FIRST EDITION 2019
REPRINT 2023

Copyright © BPB Publication, INDIA

ISBN: 978-93-88511-15-5

All Rights Reserved. No part of this publication can be stored in a retrieval system or reproduced in any form or by any means without the prior written permission of the publishers

LIMITS OF LIABILITY AND DISCLAIMER OF WARRANTY

The Author and Publisher of this book have tried their best to ensure that the programmes, procedures and functions described in the book are correct. However, the author and the publishers make no warranty of any kind, expressed or implied, with regard to these programmes or the documentation contained in the book. The author and publisher shall not be liable in any event of any damages, incidental or consequential, in connection with, or arising out of the furnishing, performance or use of these programmes, procedures and functions. Product name mentioned are used for identification purposes only and may be trademarks of their respective companies.

All trademarks referred to in the book are acknowledged as properties of their respective owners.

Distributors:

BPB PUBLICATIONS
20, Ansari Road, Darya Ganj
New Delhi-110002
Ph: 23254990/23254991

BPB BOOK CENTRE
376 Old Lajpat Rai Market,
Delhi-110006
Ph: 23861747

MICRO MEDIA
Shop No. 5, Mahendra Chambers,
150 DN Rd. Next to Capital Cinema,
V.T. (C.S.T.) Station, MUMBAI-400 001
Ph: 22078296/22078297

DECCAN AGENCIES
4-3-329, Bank Street,
Hyderabad-500195
Ph: 24756967/24756400

Published by Manish Jain for BPB Publications, 20, Ansari Road, Darya Ganj, New Delhi-110002 and Printed by Manipal Technologies Limited, Manipal

Preface

My vigorous effort towards the understanding of students and their problems in 3ds MAX will be solved after my attempt for this book. So far, my earlier book AUTOCAD 2015 REFERENCE, AUTOCAD 2017 Training Guide, AUTOCAD 2018 Training Guide and then Revit, followed by Revit 2019 have been a success for my beloved readers. As I receive positive feedbacks, and numerous people are benefitting from it, I am being more eloquent for this book with novel projects and easy language. This book carries a lot for you, if you are starting 3ds MAX 2019 for the first time. This book is extremely simple to understand and will enlighten you with the fundamentals of 3ds MAX 2019; you can easily learn 3ds MAX 2019 as it is a basic step-by-step book. The main objective of writing this book; after being inspired from my previous edition, is to make students enthusiastic about learning the concepts of 3ds MAX 2019. I wish you a great future in designing.

DESIGNING THE WORLD

Acknowledgments

While writing this book, I was constantly supported and guided by many wonderful people. Their extended support will always be priceless for me. My mother, Archana Sagar, is a woman of substance. Like any other mother in the world, her unconditional support, caring nature, never-ending faith in me, and motivation encouraged me to finally realize that I can transfer my knowledge through writing for various other people who seek the same knowledge. And, this is how my book writing began. I would like to thank my sister, Shivani Sagar, who always lovingly supports, motivates, and inspires me. Many thanks to my wife, Mansi Sagar, who is a wonderful partner; she not only understands my dreams and aspirations, but is equally involved in internalizing and living it up with me. It's wonderful how she was took on all the responsibilities so that I can get space and comfort for writing this book with dedication. She stands strong with me in all the highs and lows of my life. These two women are the sources of continuous energy that keep me going. This book is about technical skills precision and perfection in the engineering field. My special thanks to Nisha, who helped me to write this book in very short period of time, as I understand the technical aspect, but was unable to express; she assisted me with lucid language for the book. I would like to express my gratitude to Jyoti Chhabra who helped in researching Revit and in finalizing this project within a limited timeframe. I am thankful to Manoj Dwivedi who personally supervised, supported, and encouraged me all through this work.

Without the experiences and support from my peers and team at DUCAT, this book wouldn't be possible.

And, last but not least, thanks to *BPB Publications*.

Contents

Chapter 5: Basic Tools

Chapter 6: Advance Modeling Tools

CHAPTER-1

Introduction and Overview

WHAT IS 3DS MAX?

3Ds max is Autodesk 3D studio max software. It was launched in 1996. But before this, there was a 3Ds prototype software in 1988 which was run on MS dos. Basically, it is used for 3D modelling, Animation, and Graphics. It is an Autodesk product which is used for 3D modelling. Now a days, it is used in every industry Gaming, Automobile, Civil, Mechanical, Electrical, Animation, Graphics, and Visual Effects etc.

Version	Year	Operating system
3D Studio Prototype	1988	MS-DOS
3D Studio	1990	
3D Studio 2	1992	
3D Studio 3	1993	
3D Studio 4	1994	
3D Studio MAX 1.0	1996	Windows NT 3.51, Windows NT 4.0
3D Studio MAX R2	1997	Windows 95 and Windows NT 4.0
3D Studio MAX R3	1999	
Discreet 3dsmax 4	2000	Windows 98, Windows ME, Windows 2000[4]
Discreet 3dsmax 5	2002	Windows 2000 and Windows XP
Discreet 3dsmax 6	2003	
Discreet 3dsmax 7	2004	
Autodesk 3ds Max 8	2005	
Autodesk 3ds Max 9	2006	
Autodesk 3ds Max 2008	2007	Windows XP and Windows Vista
Autodesk 3ds Max 2009	2008	
Autodesk 3ds Max 2010	2009	
Autodesk 3ds Max 2011	2010	Windows XP, Windows Vista and Windows 7
Autodesk 3ds Max 2012	2011	
Autodesk 3ds Max 2013	2012	Windows XP and Windows 7
Autodesk 3ds Max 2014	2013	Windows 7
Autodesk 3ds Max 2015	2014	Windows 7 and Windows 8
Autodesk 3ds Max 2016	2015	Windows 7, Windows 8 and Windows 8.1

Version	Year	Operating system
Autodesk 3ds Max 2017	2016	Windows 7, Windows 8, Windows 8.1 and Windows 10
Autodesk 3ds Max 2018	2017	
Autodesk 3ds Max 2019	2018	

GUI OF 3DS MAX

Before doing work on 3Ds MAX, you should know about all the tools used in it that where is that tool, category of tool, and about the tab of that tool. Which are as follows:

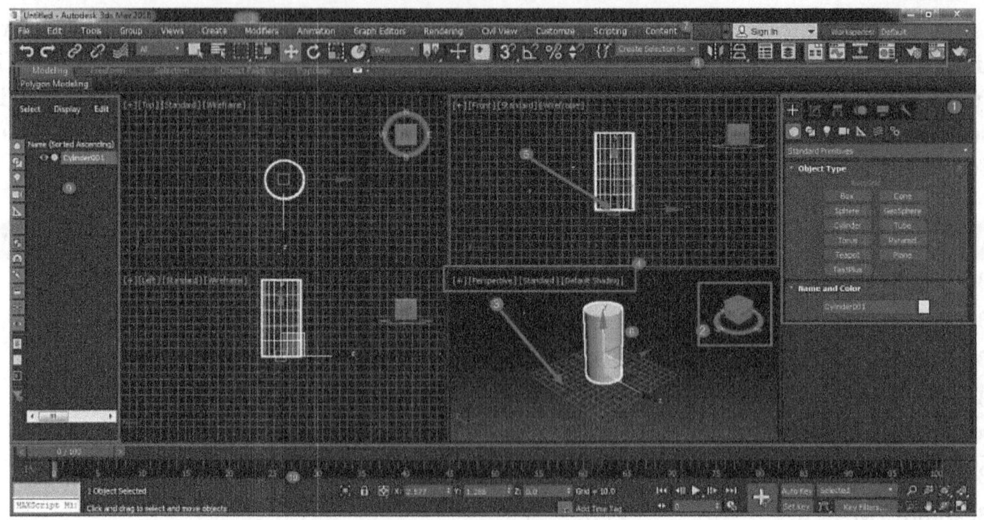

Figure 1 *3DS Max*

1. **Command panel:** It is used to create or modify the object or element. You can change or add the properties or size of an object. Or by using this, you can modify the object.
2. **View control:** It is used to see any side of an object like top side, left side or isometric view etc.
3. **Grid:** Grid works as an interface, which is used to control the position of an object.
4. **Viewport level menus:** Viewport is used to change the view or visual style of the object. By this, view of camera is shown.
5. **Axis:** Axis is used to show the axis of an object like X, Y, and Z. By which you can move, rotate, or scale the object.
6. **Element:** Element can be converted into any shape, which can be used as an object. For making any design, object is used.
7. **Menu:** All the tools of 3DS Max are opened from menu or can be used directly from here like new file, Open file, Save, to create object or to modify object. They have their different menu.
8. **Main toolbar:** Main toolbar is used for some important tools like Move, Rotate, Scale, Render or Material, which can used directly from here.

9. **Scene explorer:** It works as a layer by which any object can be filter, can be sort as many things you can do by the scene explorer. It shows the name of a particular object by which object can be easily selected.
10. **Status bar control:** Status bar is used to create animation or to control the position of an object. It is a kind of timeline, which works to control the animation.

SHORTCUT

Shortcut is used to make the working process simple and fast. By the shortcut, there is no need to go to the menu repeatedly and no need to click repeatedly on Move, Rotate or change the view etc.

Short cut key	Use
A	Toggle Angle Snap on/off.
B	Change active viewport to *Bottom* view.
c	Change active viewport to *Camera* view (there must be at least 1 camera in your scene for this command to work). If you have more than 1 camera in your scene, this will toggle between cameras.
d	Disable view (prevents view from updating; used when editing very large scenes to improve performance)
e	Rotate selected object (does not Select).
f	Change active viewport to *Front* view.
g	Toggle grid on/off.
h	Select hidden objects in select from scene dialog by name to unhide those objects.
i	Center active viewport to the mouse's position.
j	Show hide selection brackets
l	Change active viewport to "Left" view.
m	Open the Material Editor.
N	Toggle Auto Key on/off.
O	Adaptive degradation, shows objects as boxes, speed up viewport drawing in complex scenes.
P	Change active viewport to *Perspective* view.
Q	Select Object.
R	Select and Scale.
S	Toggle Snap on/off.
T	Change active viewport to *Top* view.
U	Change active viewport to *User* view.
W	Select and move.

Short cut key	Use
X	Hide/unhide gizmo.
z	Zoom Extents All Selected.
6	Particle View (v6 & 7 only).
7	Polygon Count (displayed at upper left of viewport for selected object).
8	Environment panel.
0	Render to texture
Space	Lock selection
Up arrow	Walkthrough mode
MMB	Pan view
Ctrl+MMB	2x Pan speed
Ctrl+A	Select all
Ctrl+I	Invert selection
Ctrl+V	Clone selected Object
Ctrl+C	(This is not copy!)(In perspective viewport) create target camera using the current view.
Ctrl+X	expert Mode
Ctrl+Z	Undo
Ctrl+Y	Redo
Ctrl+LMB(click)	Add clicked object to current selection
Ctrl+LMB(hold)	Marquee, Add multiple selected to current selection
Alt+LMB(click)	Remove clicked object from current selection
Alt+LMB(hold)	Marquee, Remove multiple selected from current selection
Shift+LMB(click)	Clone selected/clicked object
Shift+LMB(click+drag)	(with move selected) Clone and move selected/clicked object
Alt+MMB	Rotate View
Alt+X	X-ray view mode
Alt+Q	Isolates the selected objects
Alt+w	Maximize viewport toggle

UNIT

To change the units of the page of 3Ds MAX like Length, Breadth or height Unit is used. It is used for the unit setup of whole page so that the design must be in proper units like Meter, Millimeter, Inch or Feet etc.

Step 1: First of all, right click on Customize menu, then click on units setup.

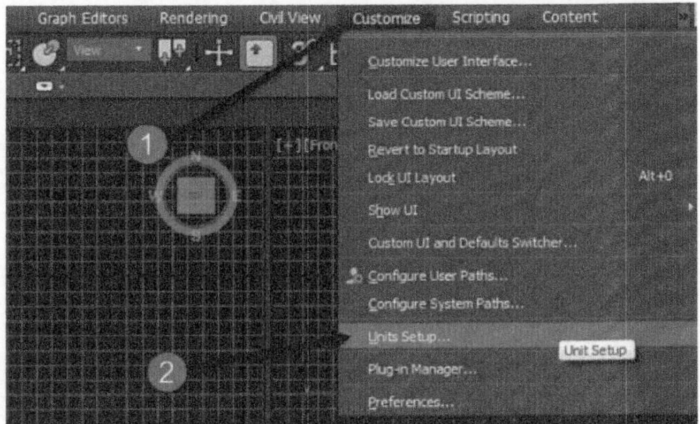

Figure 2 *UNIT Setup command*

Step 2: After that, select any type unit like Metric or US Standard.

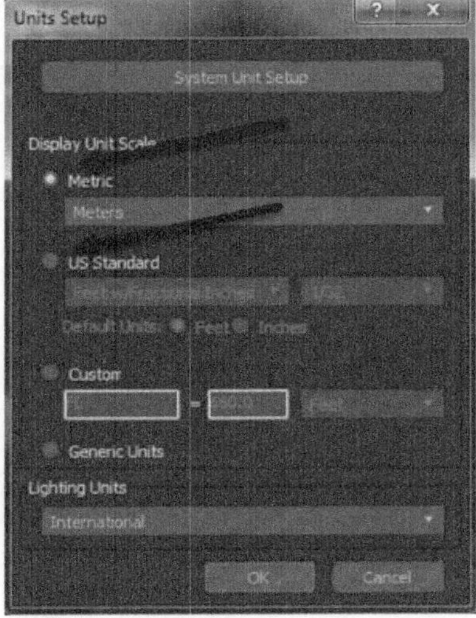

Figure 3 *Unit Type*

MOUSE USE (MOVE, ZOOM AND ROTATE)

Use the mouse to rotate, move, zoom in, and zoom out page. For the correct use of the mouse, it is necessary to have a scroll button in the mouse.

1. **Move or Pan:** Press scroll button + move the Mouse.
2. **Zoom out:** Scroll up for zoom out.
3. **Zoom in:** Scroll down for zoom in.
4. **Orbit or Rotate:** Press scroll + Alt + Mouse move.

Figure 4 *Mouse Button*

■ Viewport Label Menus

The General Viewport label menus (+) in the upper-left corner of each viewport provides the options for overall viewport display or activation. There are three types of tabs in it. To set Viewport, Visual style, and View.

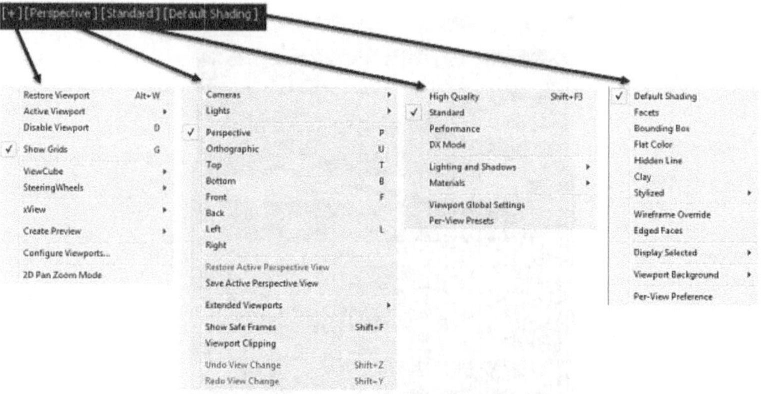

Figure 5 *View port type*

■ ViewCube

The View Cube 3D navigation control, provides visual feedback of the current orientation of a viewport. You can easily see any side of any object. Such as front, back, left, etc…

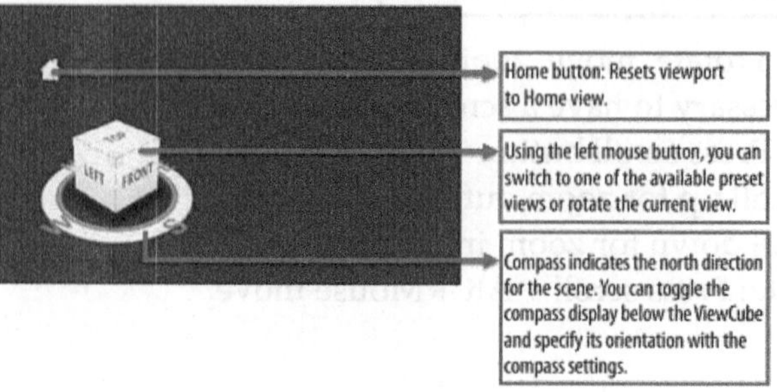

Figure 6 *ViewCube*

■ Selecting Objects

3ds Max has a wide variety of object types, such as geometry, lights, cameras, and bones, among others. 3ds Max can select objects individually, by group and by name. Objects can be selected individually or in groups by using the mouse. When left clicking an object selects it, left-clicking and dragging selects a region. Holding the *Ctrl* key while selecting ads to a selection, and holding the *Alt* key removes from the selection.

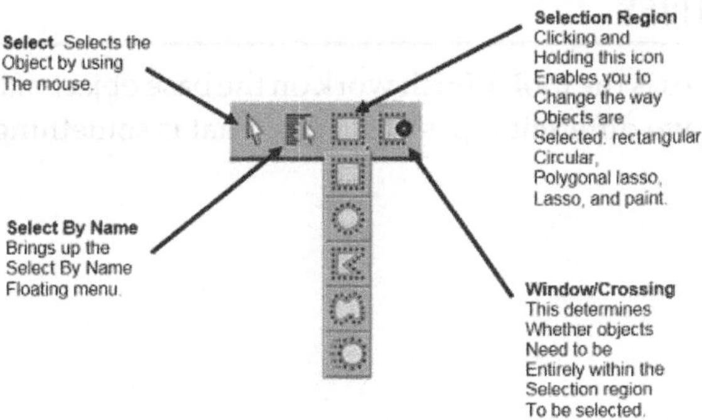

Figure 7 *Selecting tool option*

■ Transforming Objects

Selected objects can be moved, rotated, and scaled. These transforms can be accessed by using the icons on the main toolbar or by pressing the hot keys W (Move), E (Rotate), and R (Scale).

Each transform uses a color-coded gizmo. Red transforms along the X-axis, green along the Y-axis, and blue along the Z-axis. Whichever axis you want to use, click on that axis and drag it.

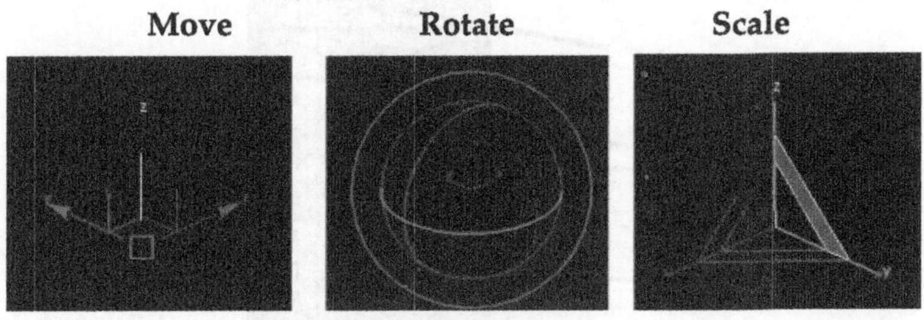

Figure 8 *Move Rotate Scale Icon*

CHAPTER-2

Create-Geometry

STANDARD PRIMITIVES

Standard Primitives is the tool, Which work on the base object of the design. They are mostly used. They have different types of shapes. That is something like the following:

1. Box
2. Cone
3. Sphere
4. Geosphere
5. Cylinder
6. Tube
7. Torus
8. Pyramid
9. Teapot
10. Plane
11. Textplus

To create any object of Standard Primitives:

- Create → Geometry → Standard Primitives → Click on any object, which you want.

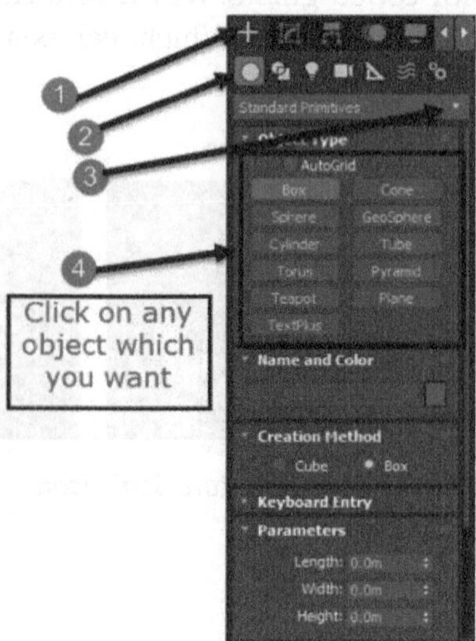

Figure 1 *Standard Primitives tool option*

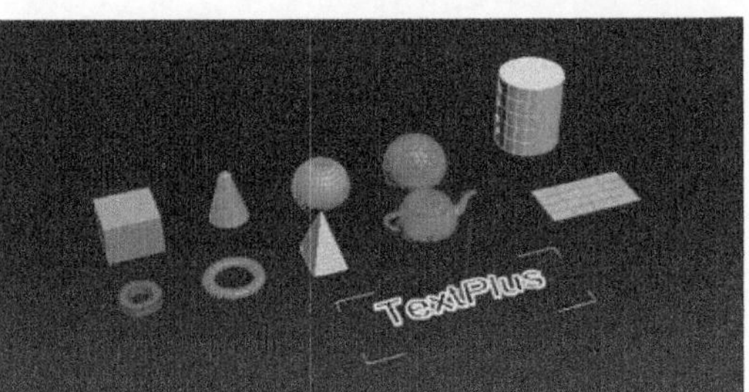

Figure 2 *Standard primitives*

Note: If you have to change the dimension of an object. First of all, select object then click modify tab.

Step 1: Select the object.

Step 2: Click on the modify tab.

Step 3: Specify dimension like: Length, width, Segment etc.

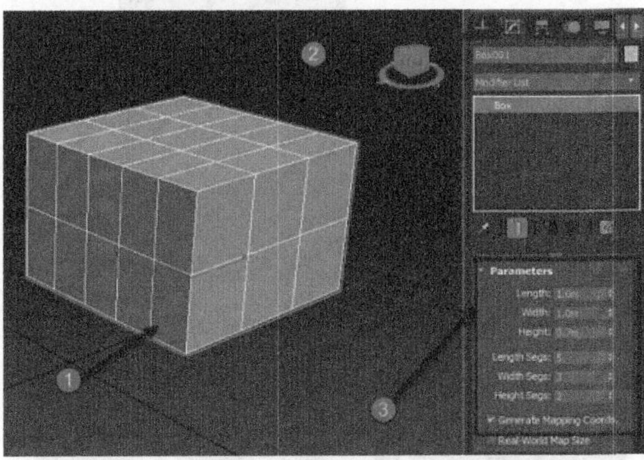

Figure 3 *How to change the dimension.*

EXTENDED PRIMITIVES

Extended primitives is use to create an advance object. There are many types of a shape in it too, which can be changed with the help of modifier tool. These objects are complex. Which work in advance objects in design. And with its help, some design is quickly created. Because it does not have to make some objects due to this. That is something like the following:

1. Hedra
2. Torus knot
3. Chamfer box
4. Chamfer cylinder
5. Oil tank
6. Capsule

7. Spindle
8. L-Extrusion
9. Gengon
10. C-Extrusion
11. Ringwave
12. Hose
13. Prism

To create any object of Standard Primitives:

➢ Create ➡ Geometry ➡ Extended Primitives ➡ Click on any object, which you want.

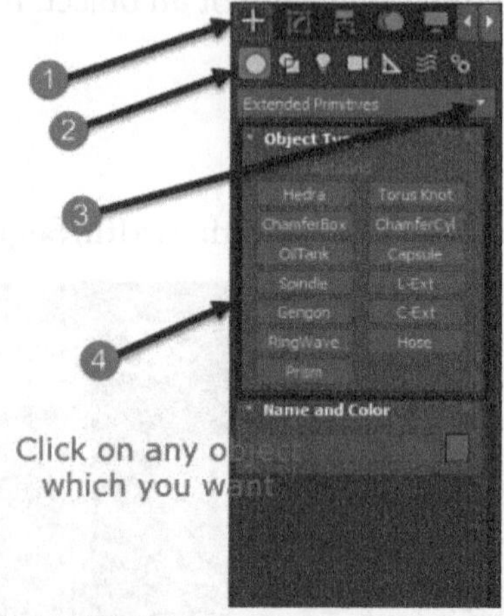

Figure 4 *Extended Primitives tool option*

Figure 5 *Extended Primitives*

Note: If you have to change the dimension or parameters of an object. First of all, select object then click modify tab.

Step 1: Select the object.

Step 2: Click on **modify** tab.

Step 3: Click on the parameters which you want.

Figure 6 *How to change the dimension*

AEC OBJECT

You use AEC tools to create objects such as walls, doors, windows, and stairs, among others. AEC tools are mostly useful in 3ds Max Design but they can also be used in 3ds Max.

1. Railing
2. Wall
3. Door
4. Stair
5. Window

➢ Create ➞ **AEC Objects** ➞ Click on any object, which you want.

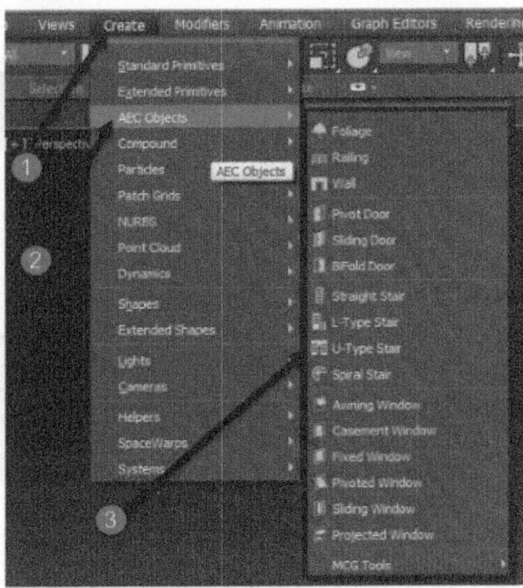

Figure 7 *AEC objects tool option*

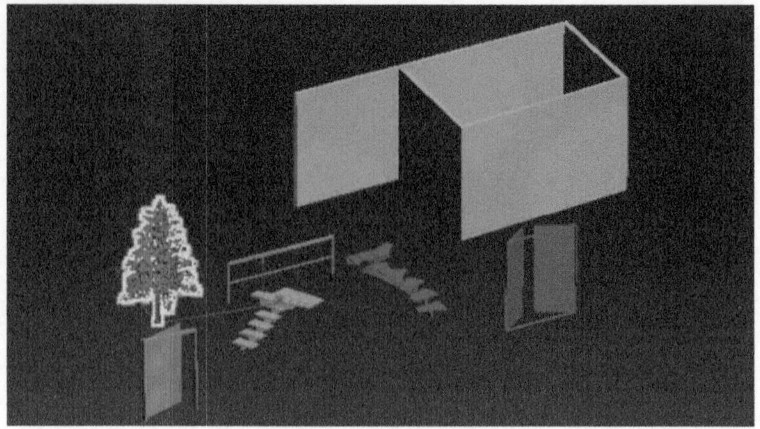

Figure 8 *AEC objects*

COMPOUND OBJECTS

Compound Objects in 3ds Max are tools, not physical objects in the sense of a Standard primitive, for example Compound Objects use two or more existing objects, 2D or 3D, and combine them to edit the form of one or the other into a new single object.

■ Morph

If both the objects are of same kind but their parameters change and their parameters have to do the same, then use the morph tool. But the objects should be of the same kind. Like two boxes but their parameters change. So use the Morph tool to do them in a way.

Step 1: First of all, create two boxes.

Figure 9 *Create two boxes.*

Step 2: Select a box and right click on the mouse. Then click on convert to: convert to editable poly.

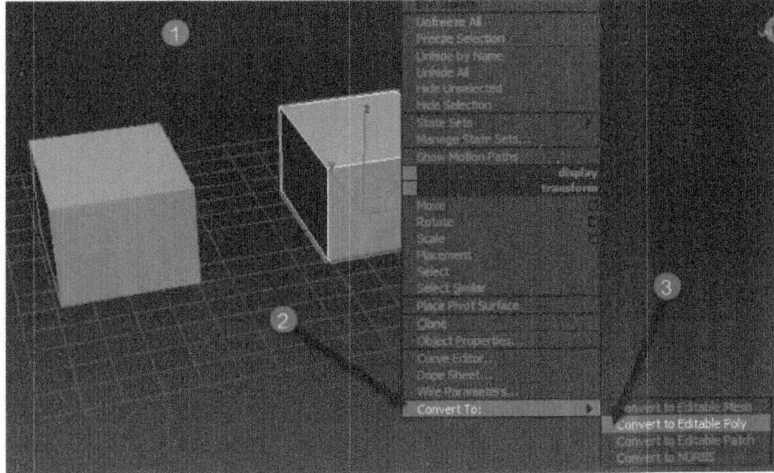

Figure 10 *Convert to editable poly*

Step 3: Click on move tool and click on selection vertex. Then select some vertex of box.

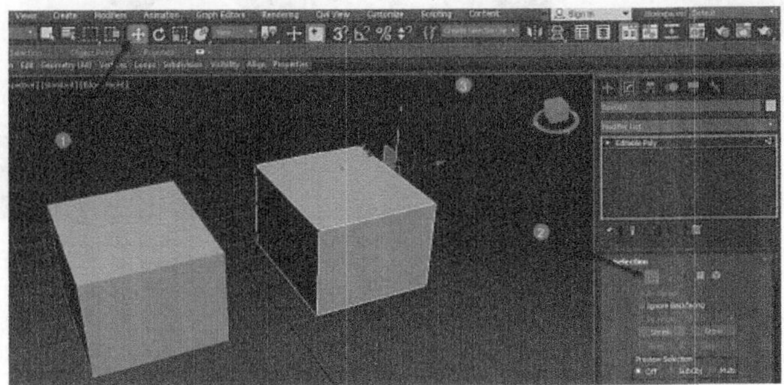

Figure 11 *Select vertex for move*

Step 4: Click on z-axis and drag up side.

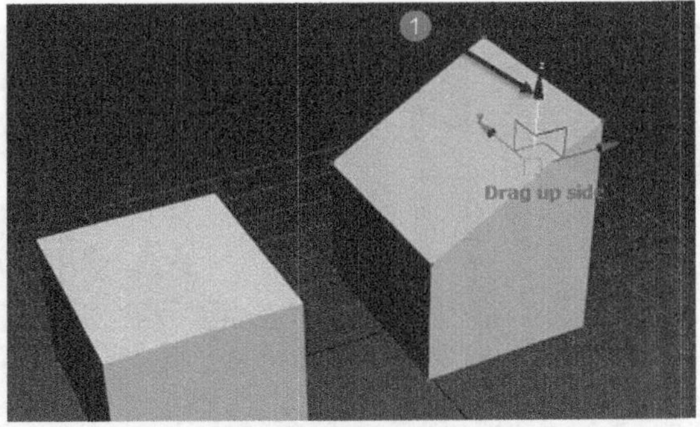

Figure 12 *Drag Z axis for move vertex*

Step 5: After that, select first box and click on morph tool.

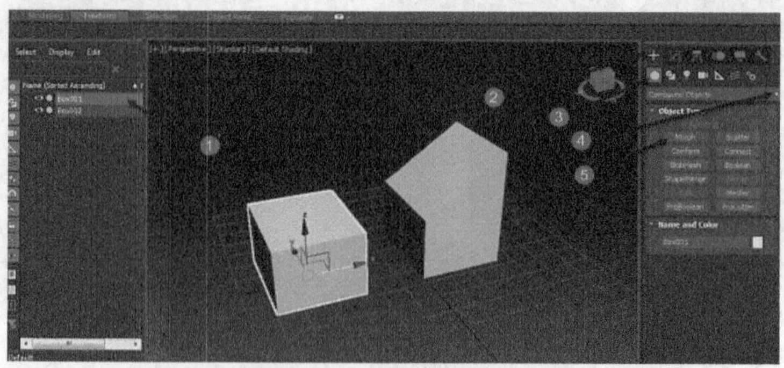

Figure 13 *Click morph tool*

Step 6: Click on **Pick Target** button and pick on reference box.

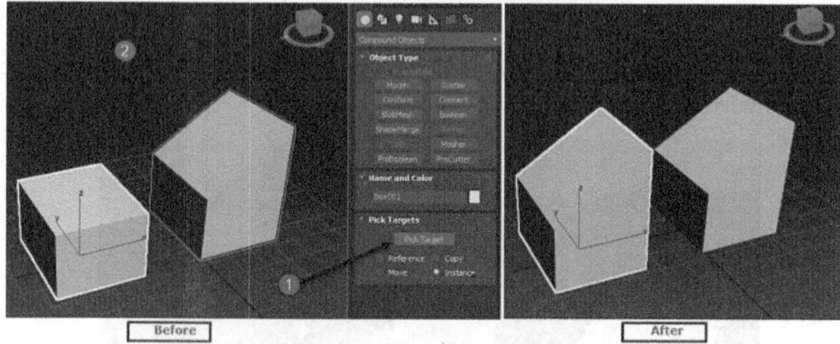

Figure 14 *use morph tool*

Scatter

Use scatter tool to arrange any object randomly on the outer surface. Like if you have to plant a lot of trees on a plane. So use the scatter tool.

Step 1: First of all, create a plane and a tree.

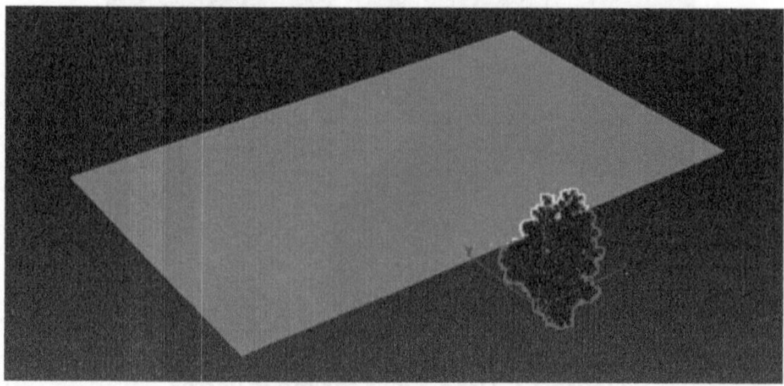

Figure 15 *Plan and tree*

Step 2: Select tree and click on scatter tool.

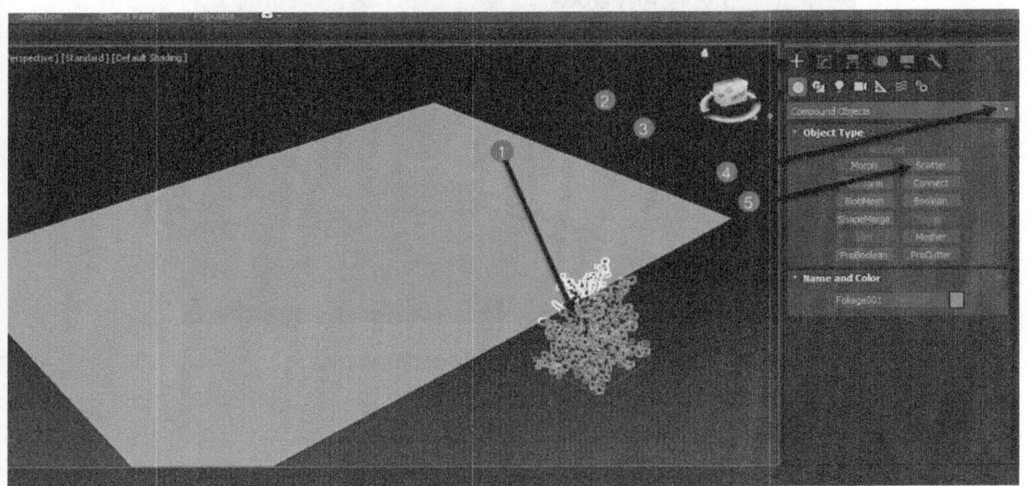

Figure 16 *Select scatter tool*

Step 3: Click on **Pick Distribution Object** button and pick on plane. Then Specify duplicate number.

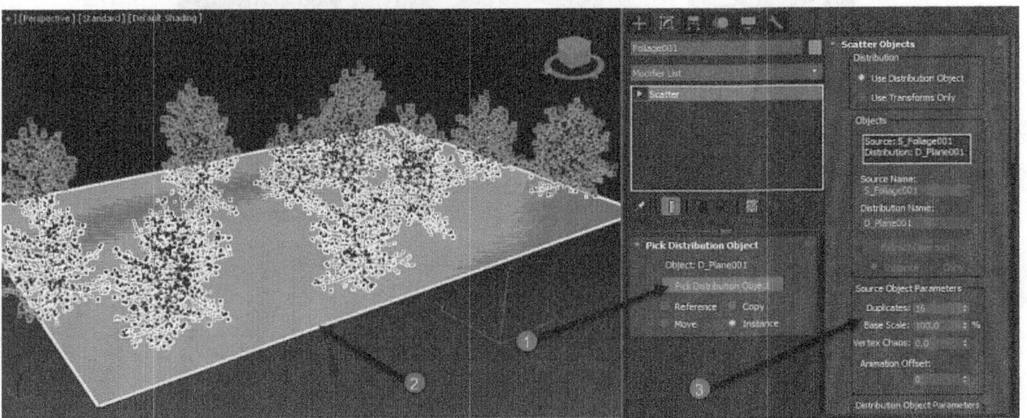

Figure 17 *Use scatter tool.*

■ Conform

Use the Confirm Tool to attach a Surface to another Surface and change it as Shape in the same way.

Step 1: First of all, create a plane and apply wave tool.

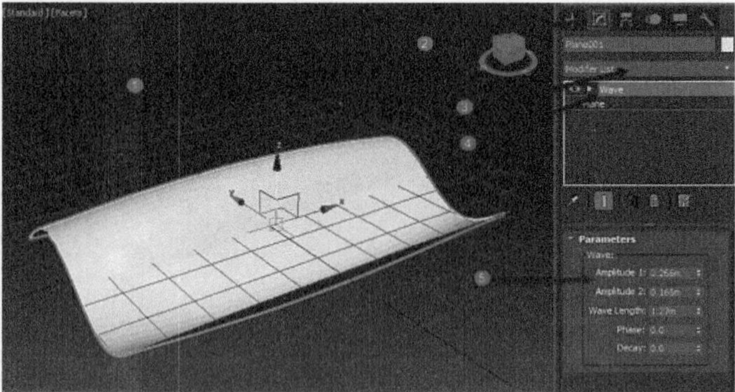

Figure 18 *Apply wave tool on plane.*

Step 2: Create a tube and convert editable poly.

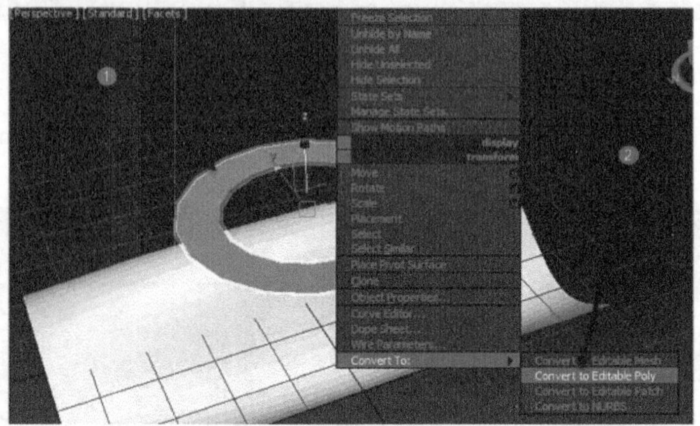

Figure 19 *Convert to editable poly of tube*

Step 3: Select tube and click on conform tool.

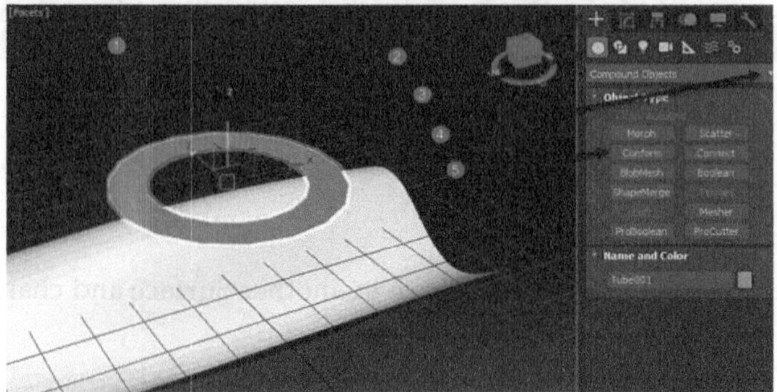

Figure 20 *Click on conform tool*

Step 4: Click on pick wrap to object button and pick on plane.

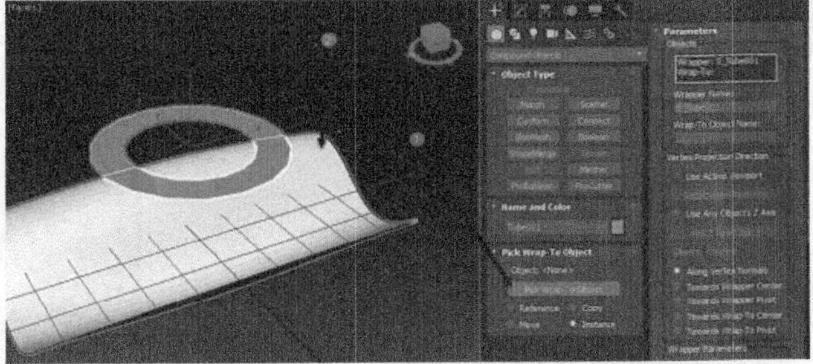

Figure 21 *Pick on plane*

Step 5: After that, click on hide tick.

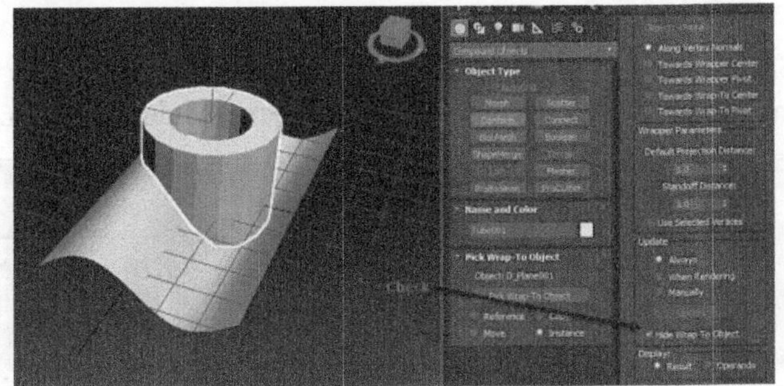

Figure 22 *Finale use of conform*

■ Connect

Use Connect Tool to connect any two objects together. The connect tool joins the object by connecting it to their open area.

Step 1: First of all, create two object like box. Then convert editable poly.

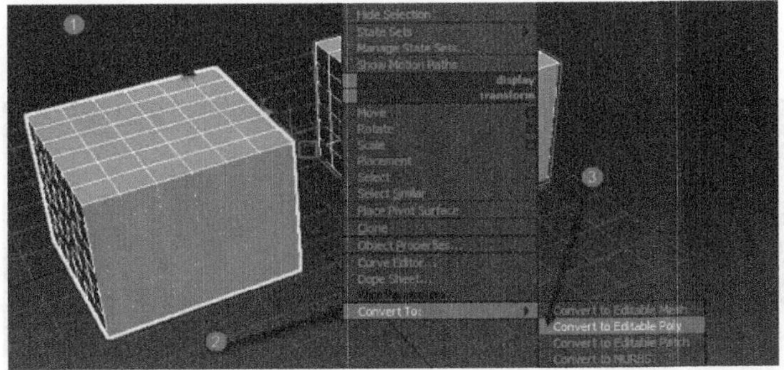

Figure 23 *Convert to editable poly of box*

Step 2: Click on selection face button and then select a face of the box. Then press **Delete** button.

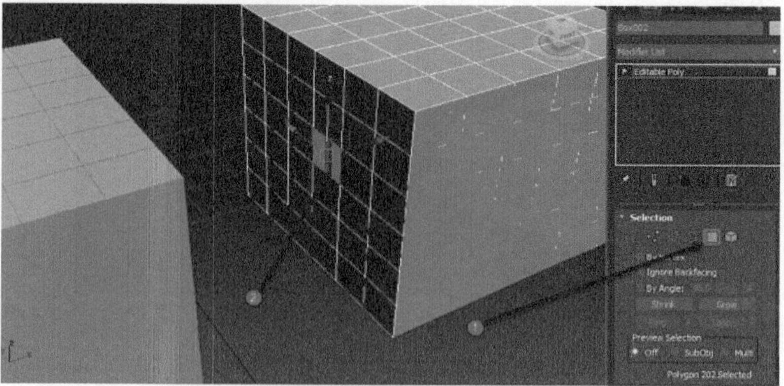

Figure 24 *Select face for delete*

Step 3: (Same step 2 repeat but on second box) Click on selection face button and then select a face of box. Then press delete button.

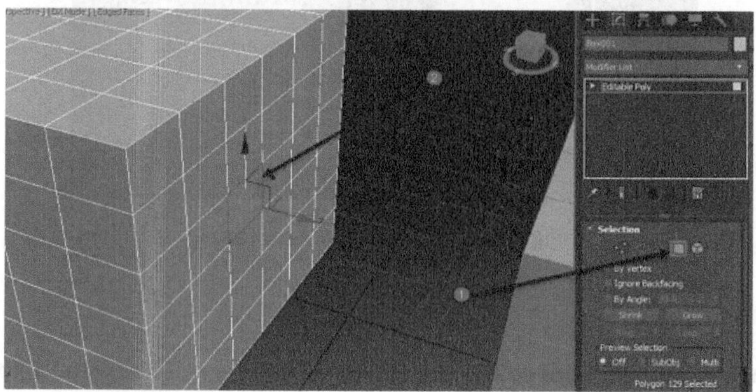

Figure 25 *Select face for delete*

Step 4: After that, select first box and click on connect tool. Then click on pick operand button and pick second box.

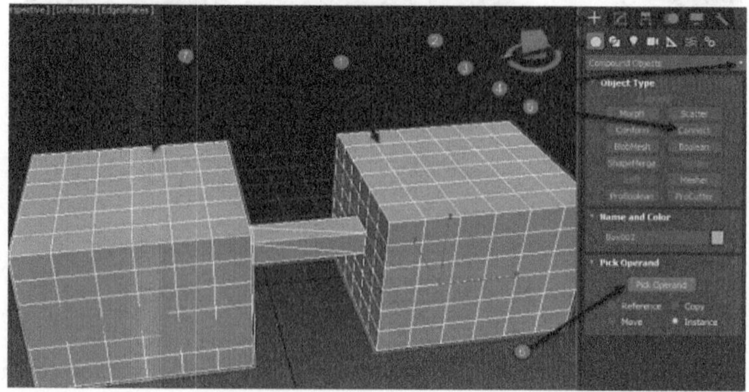

Figure 26 *Use of connect tool*

■ Blobmesh

Use the blobmesh tool to convert point to blobmesh. Like using blobmesh tools for snow or rain effects.

Step 1: First of all, create a snow with particle systems. And drag timeline right side.

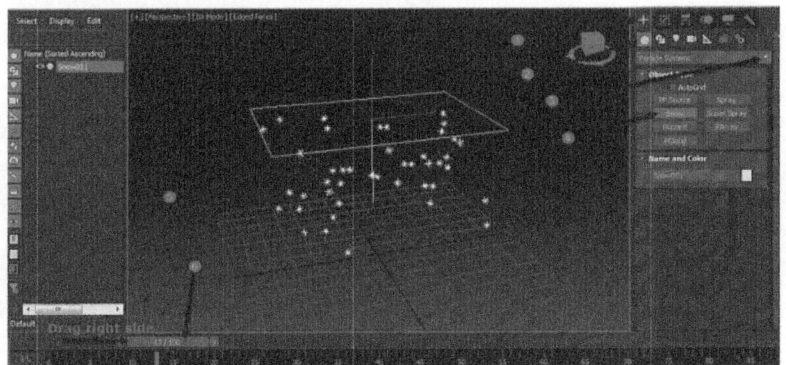

Figure 27 *Create particle system*

Step 2: Create a blobmesh.

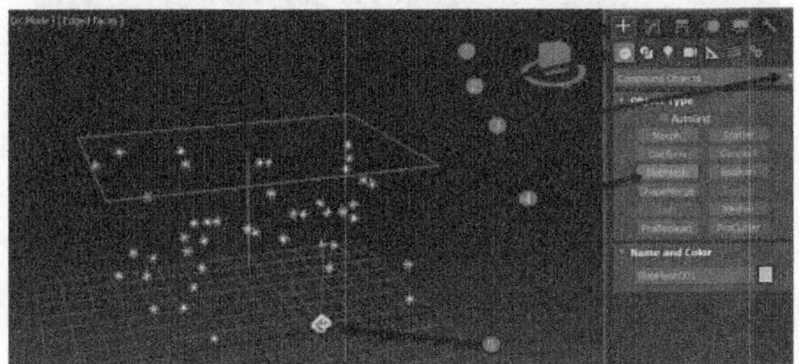

Figure 28 *Click on blobmesh tool*

Step 3: Click on modify tab and click on pick button. Then pick on plane of snow.

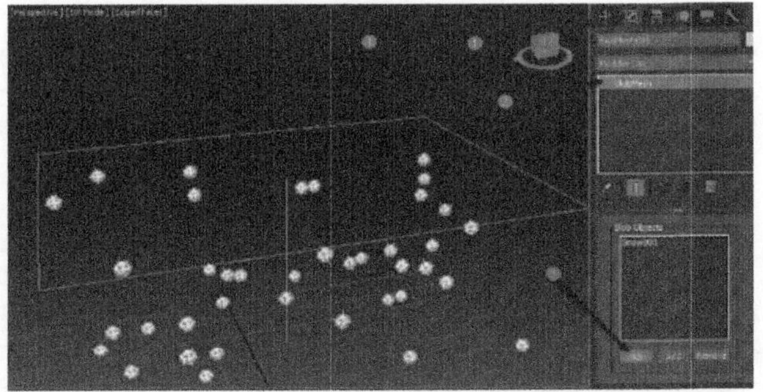

Figure 29 *use of blobmesh*

■ Boolean

Boolean tools are used to cut, join, or even merge an object with another object. It has many options. Such as subtract, merge, and union etc.

Step 1: First of all, create a box and a sphere. But both objects are intersecting each other.

Figure 30 *two object for intersect*

Step 2: Select box and click on Boolean tool.

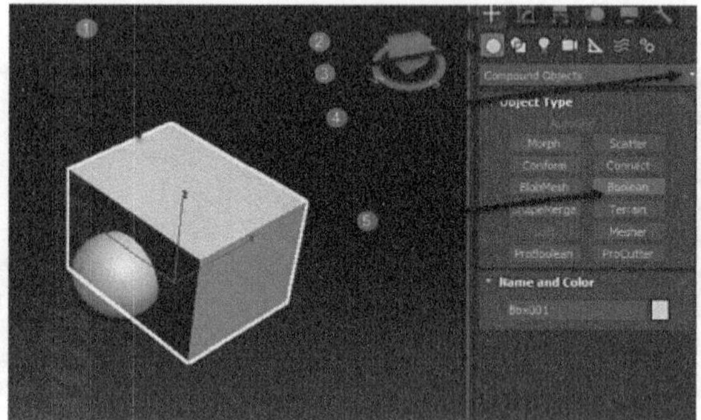

Figure 31 *Click on boolean tool*

Step 3: Click on subtract option and click on add operands button. Then pick on sphere.

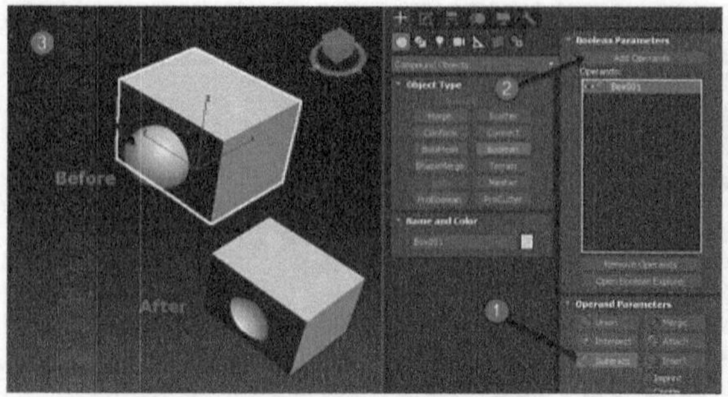

Figure 32 *use subtract option*

■ ShapeMerge

The shape merge is used to print any shape on an object. Like a box to print an ellipsis shape. Then use the shape merge.

Step 1: First of all, create a box and ellipse. Use shape tools to create ellipse.

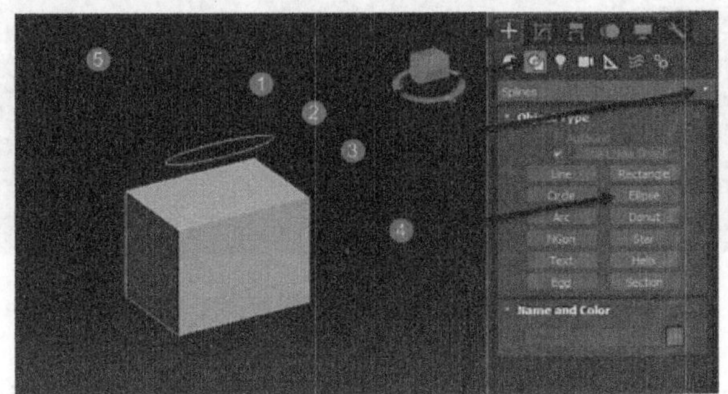

Figure 33 *create a box and ellipse*

Step 2: Select box and click on Shape merge tool. Then click on pick Shape button and pick on ellipse.

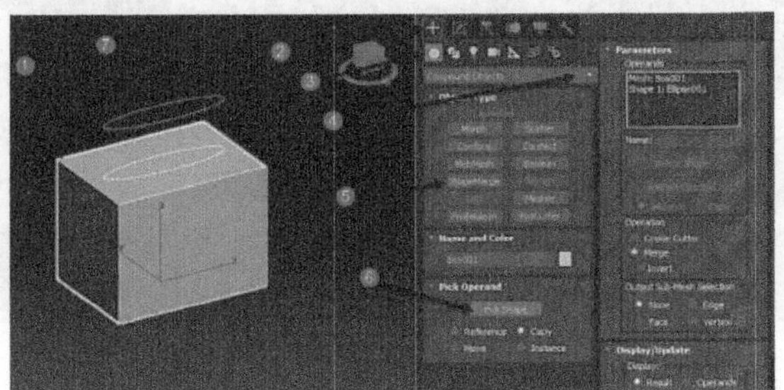

Figure 34 *click on shape merge tool*

■ Terrain

To produce a terrain, you select editable splines representing elevation contours and then click Terrain, whereupon 3ds Max generates a mesh surface over the contours.

Step 1: First of all, create three smooth line. Use shape tools to create line.

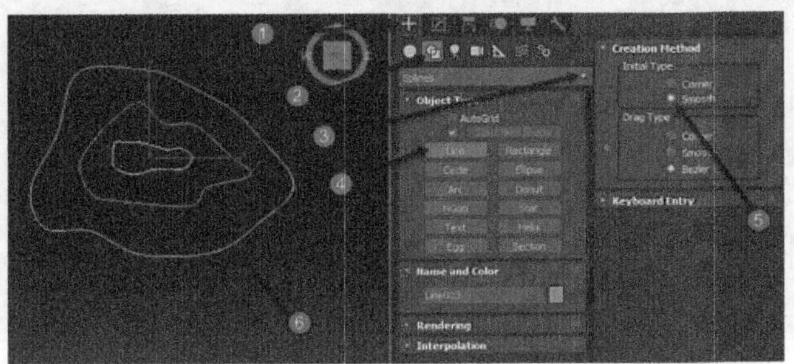

Figure 35 *Create line*

Step 2: Select all spline one by one and move in the top side with move tool.

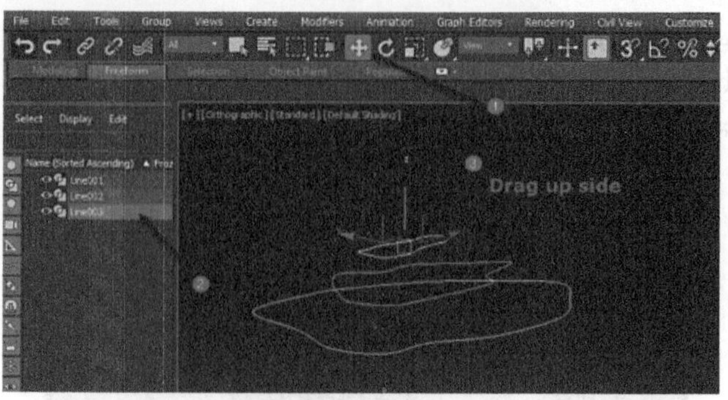

Figure 36 *Drag up side*

Step 3: Select a line and click on terrain tool. Then click on pick operand button and select all spline one by one.

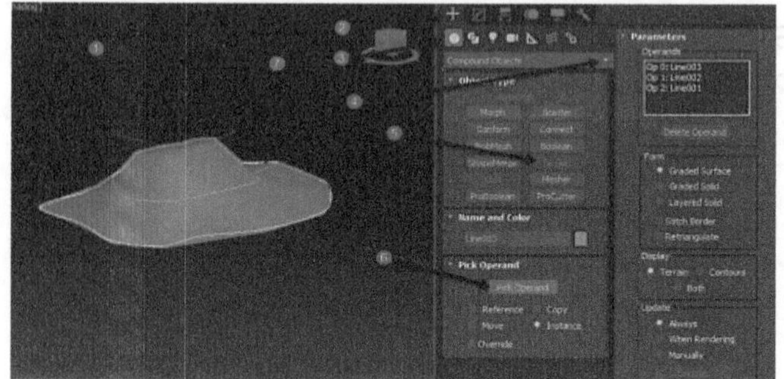

Figure 37 *Select all line and use terrain tool*

■ Loft

The use of the loft tool is to convert the path to a profile shape. It can also use one or more profiles.

Step 1: First of all, create a helix. Use shape tools to create Helix.

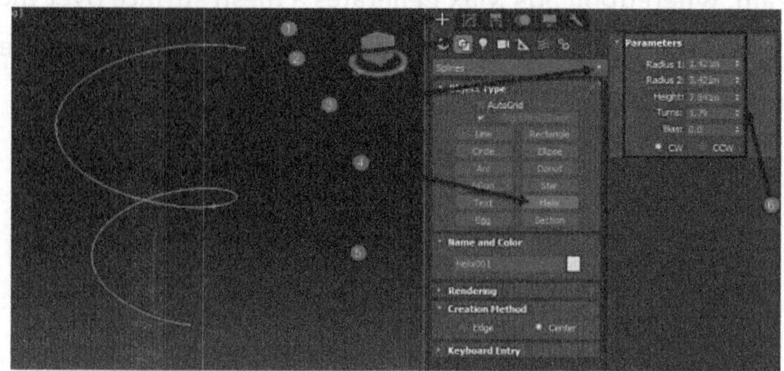

Figure 38 *Create helix*

Step 2: Create a circle and a star, use shape tools to create them.

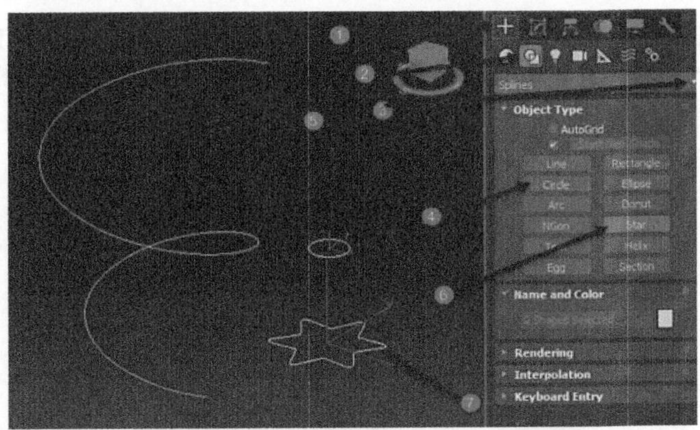

Figure 39 *Create circle and star*

Step 3: Select helix and click on the loft tool. Then click on get shape button and pick on circle.

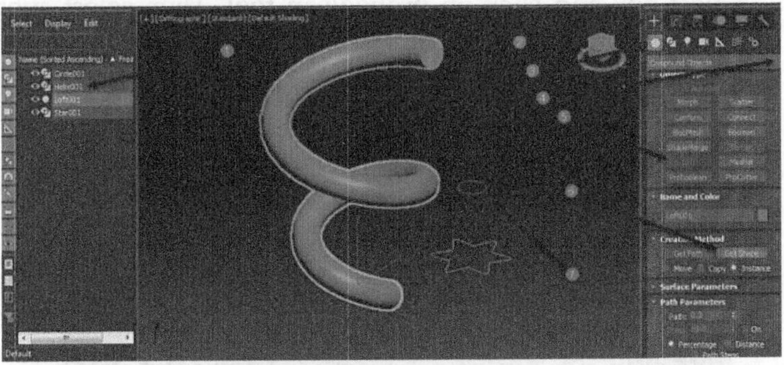

Figure 40 *use loft*

Step 4: Specify path parameters (100) and again click on the get shape button. Then pick on star.

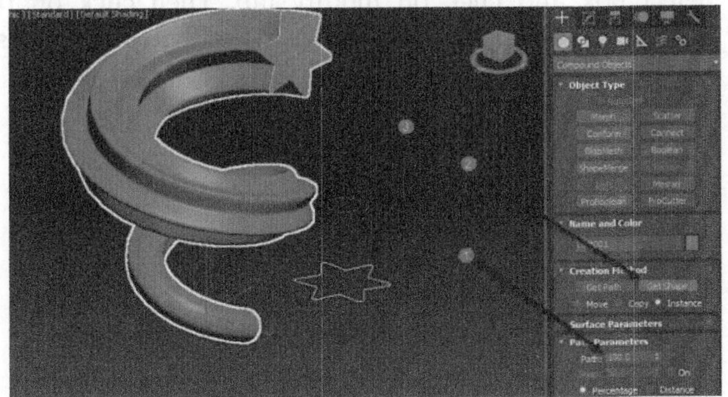

Figure 41 *Get shape*

■ Proboolean

Cut any part in any object or merge part. So, let's do the Proboolean Tool. The object to be cut or merged in the second object is moved. And intersect both of them, and then use the proboolean tool.

Step 1: First of all, create a box and a sphere.

Figure 42 *create a box and sphere*

Step 2: Select box and click on proboolean tool. Then select subtract option and click on start picking button. After that, pick on sphere.

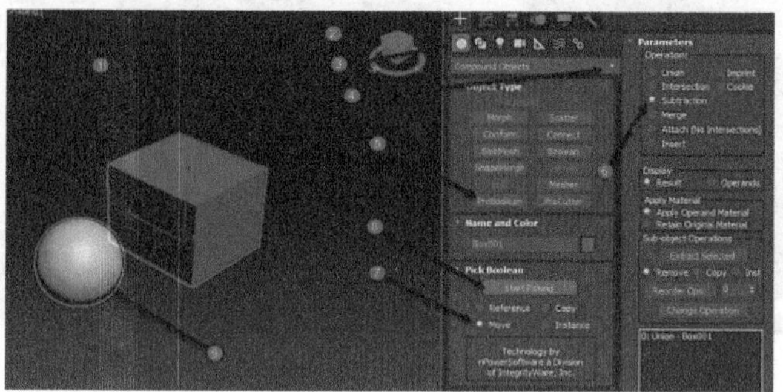

Figure 43 *Use of proboolean*

Step 3: Select box and click on modify tab. Then click on flip button of proboolean and click on operands. After that, drag X-axis.

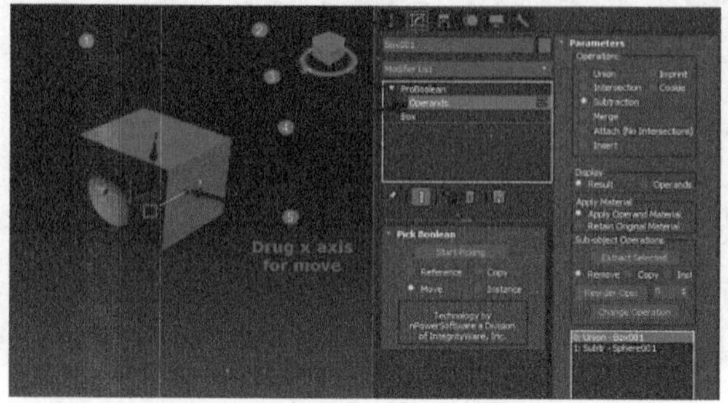

Figure 44 *Use subtract option*

■ Procutter

The ProCutter Compound object lets you perform specialized Boolean operations, primarily for the purpose of breaking apart or subdividing volumes. ProBoolean, ProCutter, and the Quadify Mesh modifier can re-mesh planar surfaces using a quadrilateral meshing algorithm.

Step 1: First of all, create a box and two plane. As given in the lower image. Keep that way or as you like.

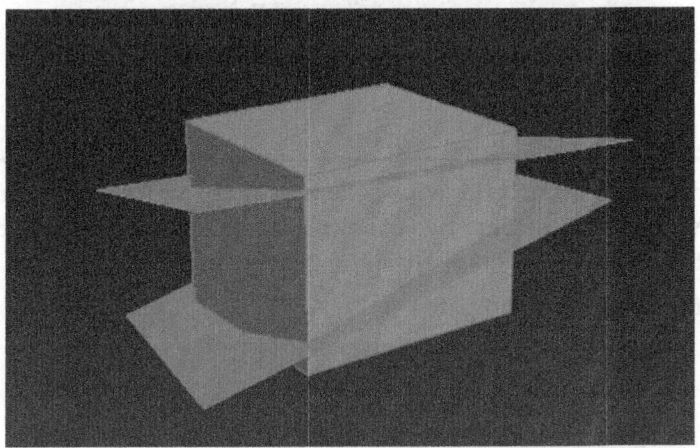

Figure 45 *create a box and two plane*

Step 2: Select a plan and click on procutter tool. Then click on pick cutter object button and select other plane.

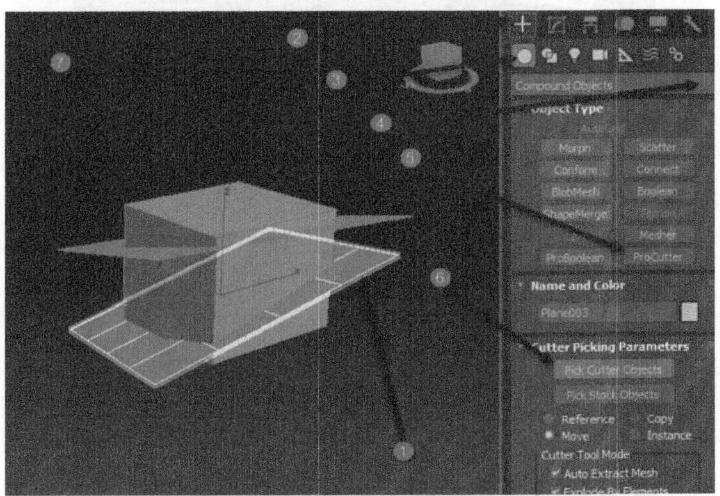

Figure 46 *Click on procutter tool*

Step 3: Select some options as given image like 2nd, 3rd option and click on pick stock objects. Then pick on box.

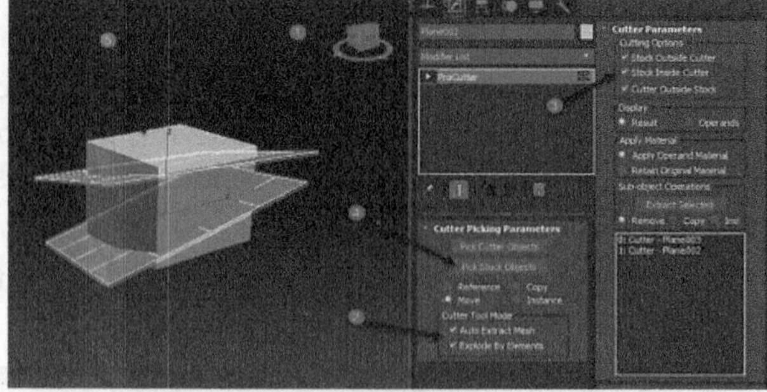

Figure 47 *use of procutter tool*

QUAD PATCH

Quad patch creates a flat grid with a default of 36 visible rectangular facets. A hidden line divides each facet into two triangular faces for a total of 72 faces. The plane can be converted into a curve shape from the quad patch.

Step 1: First of all, create a quad patch.

Figure 48 *Quad patch*

Step 2: Select quad patch and click on the right button of mouse. Then click on convert editable patch.

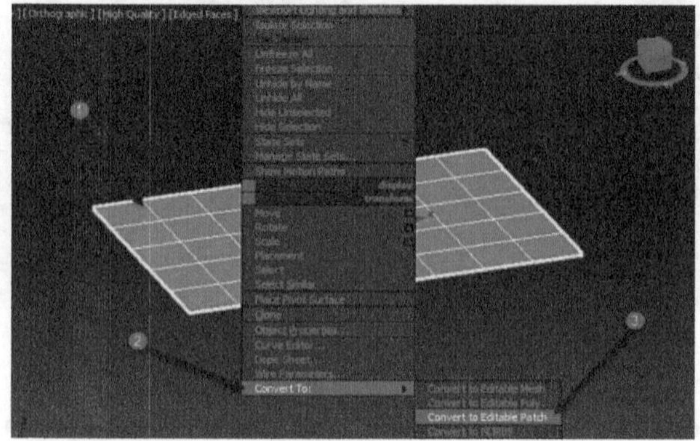

Figure 49 *Convert editable patch*

Step 3: Set up the orthographic view. Then select vertex mode and select some vertex as it has been given in the image.

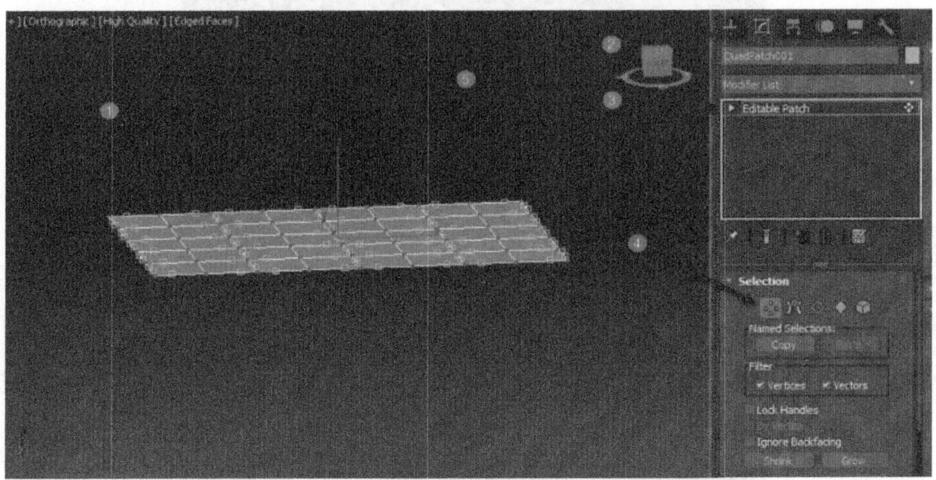

Figure 50 *Select vertex*

Step 4: Click on move tool and move Z-axis up side.

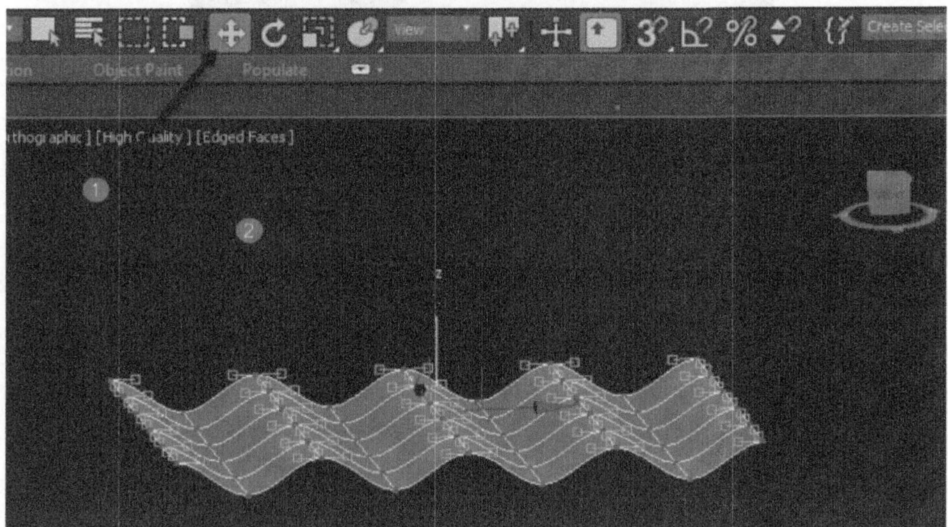

Figure 51 *Drag vertex*

NURBS POINT SURFACE

Non-uniform rational basis spline (NURBS) is a mathematical model commonly used in computer graphics for generating and representing curves and surfaces. NURBS surfaces can represent, in a compact form, simple geometrical shapes.

Step 1: Create point surface.

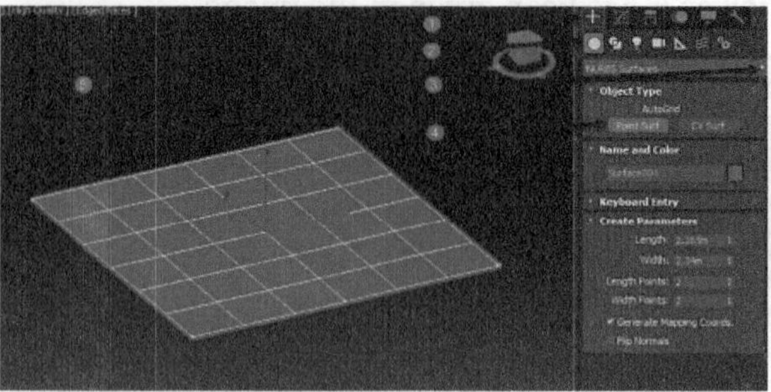

Figure 52 *create point surface*

Step 2: Select point surface and click on modify tab. Then select nurbs surface point and click on row point of selection options.

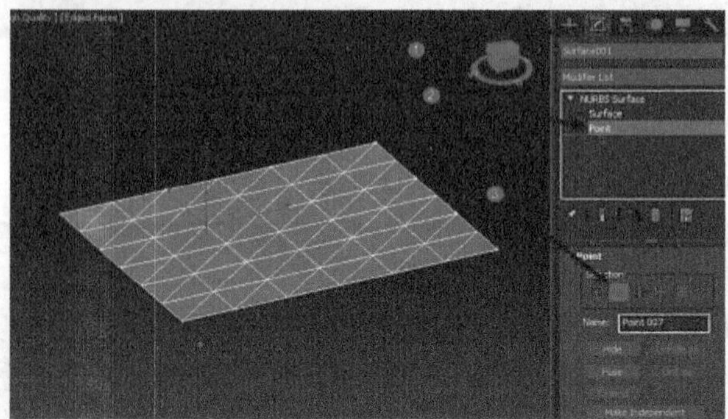

Figure 53 *select nurbs point*

Step 3: Select move tool and click on point of surface. Then move Z-axis upside.

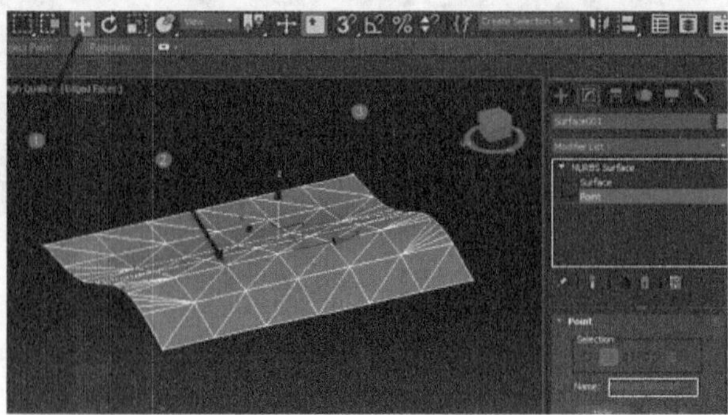

Figure 54 *Move Z axis*

CHAPTER-3

Create-Shape

SPLINE

Spline means the special line. With Spline, we can create 2D objects. Such as line, circle, rectangle, polygon etc.

1. Line
2. Rectangle
3. Circle
4. Ellipse
5. Arc
6. Donut
7. Ngon
8. Star
9. Text
10. Helix
11. Egg
12. Section

To create any shape of Spline.

- Create ➡ Shape ➡ Spline ➡ Click on any shape, which you want.

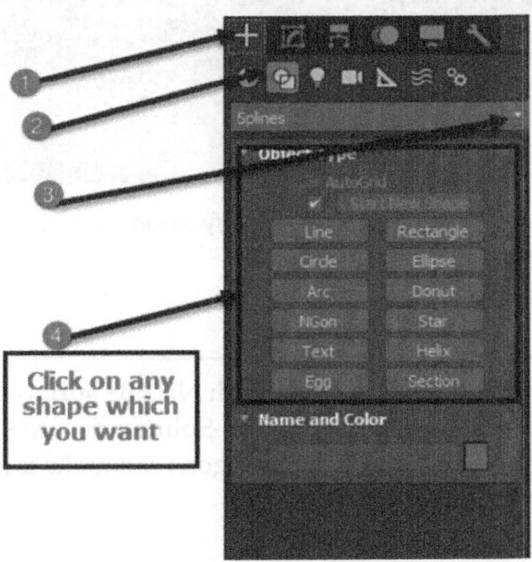

Figure 1 *Spline shape tool option*

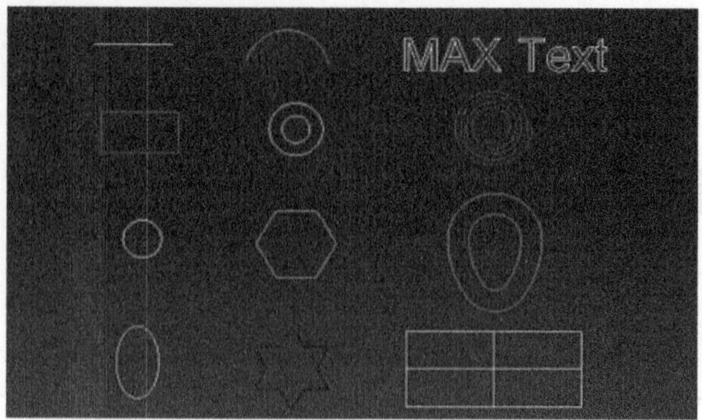

Figure 2 *Spline shape*

Note: If you have to change the dimension of any shape first of all, select the shape and then click on modify tab.

Step 1: Select shape.

Step 2: Click on modify tab.

Step 3: Specify dimension like: Radius and sides.

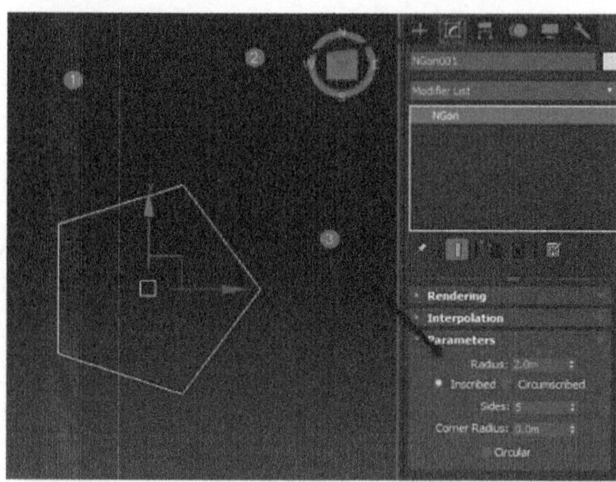

Figure 3 *Modify NGon*

NURBS CURVES

One way of modeling in 3ds Max is with NURBS surfaces and curves. NURBS, which stands for Non-Uniform Rational B-Splines, is an industry standard for designing and modeling surfaces. Using polygons can make it more difficult to create complex curved surfaces.

Step 1: Click on point curves tool.

Step 2: Pick one by one point after that pick start point for close.

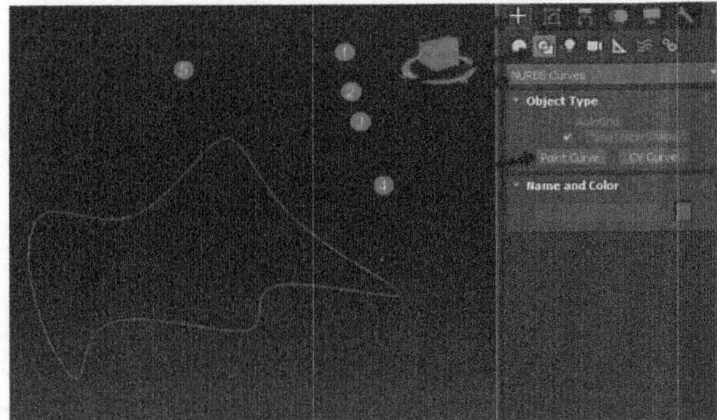

Figure 4 *Nurbs curve*

EXTENDED SPLINES

Use Extended Spline to make steel angle shape. There are different types of shapes in it. That's something like the following:

1. Wrectangle
2. Channel
3. Angle
4. Tee
5. Wide flange

To create any shape of extended splines.

➢ Create Shape ➞ Extended spline ➞ Click on any extended shape, which you want.

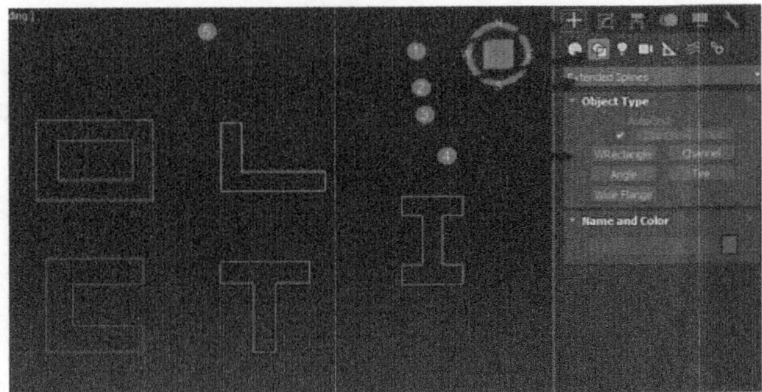

Figure 5 *Extended spline*

CHAPTER-4

Modify-Object Space Modifiers

AFFECT REGION

The Affect Region modifier is a surface modeling tool, primarily used with vertex sub-object selections while surface modeling. With Affect Region, transforming a selection of vertices can also transform vertices in the region that surrounds the selection.

Step 1: Create a plane.

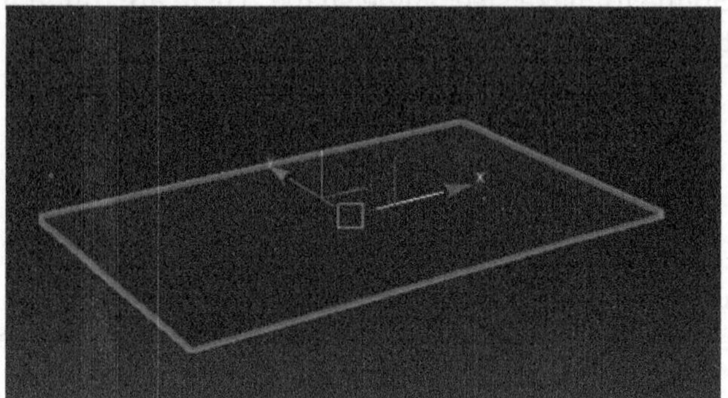

Figure 1 *Plane*

Step 2: Select plane and click modify tab then select affect region tool.

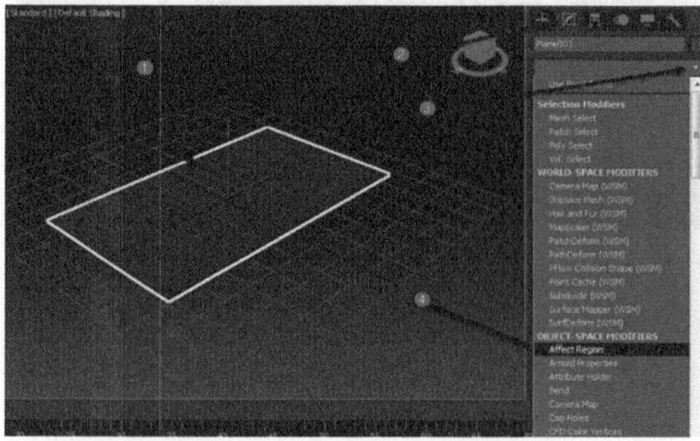

Figure 2 *Select affect region tool*

Step 3: Select affect region point and move up side. Then set parameters.

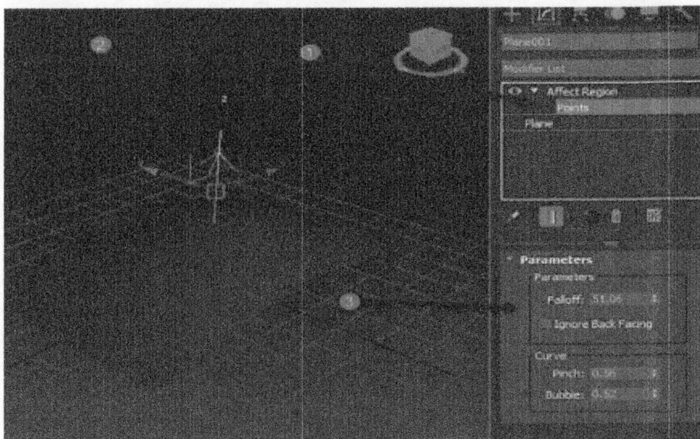

Figure 3 *Use of affect region*

BEND

Use the band tool to fold any object. But it is necessary to have a segment in the object.

Step 1: Create a box with some segments.

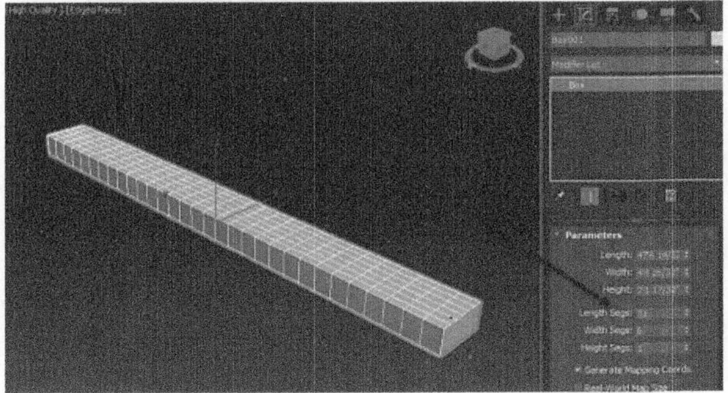

Figure 4 *Box with segments*

Step 2: Select the box and click on bend tool.

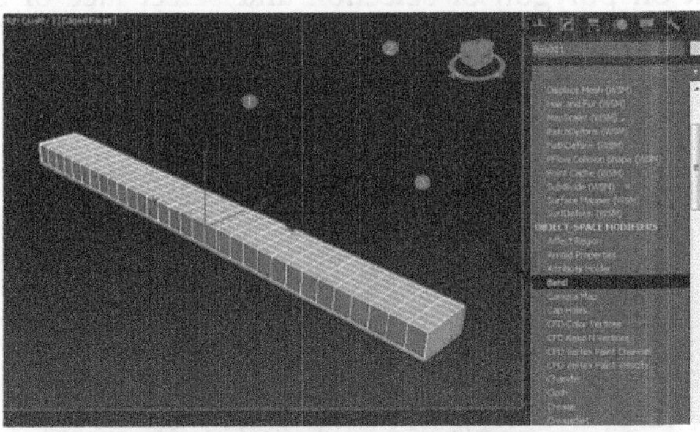

Figure 5 *Select bend tool*

Step 3: Click on Y-axis and specify angle.

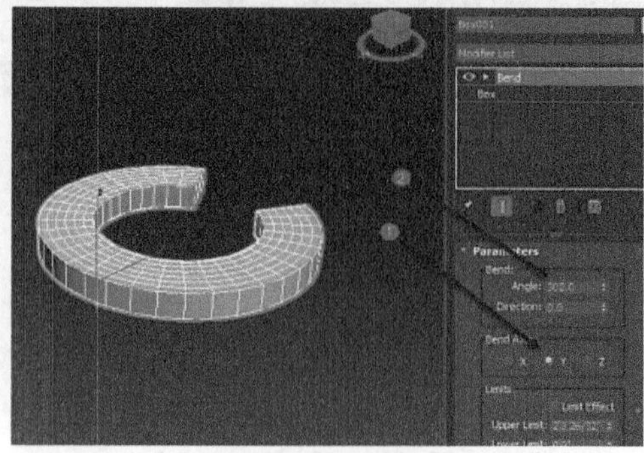

Figure 6 *Specify angle*

CAP HOLES

The Cap Holes modifier builds faces in the holes in a mesh object. A hole is defined as a loop of edges, each of which has only one face.

Step 1: Create a sphere and convert editable poly.

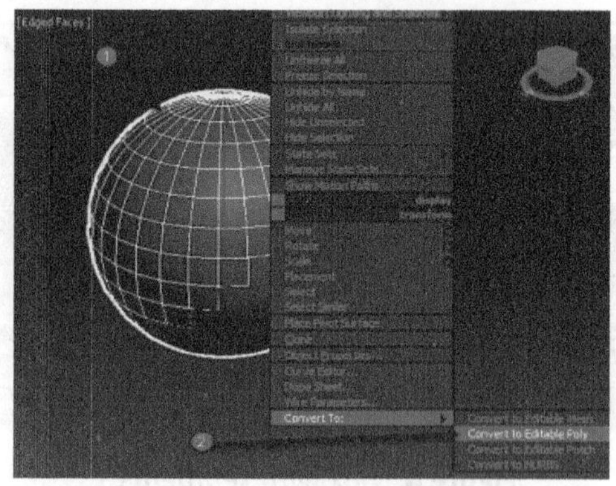

Figure 7 *Convert editable poly*

Step 2: Click on polygon of selection and select face of sphere. After that, delete it.

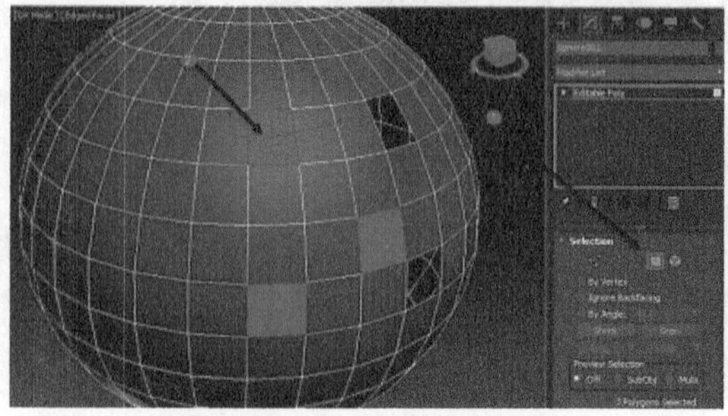

Figure 8 *Select face*

Step 3: Click on the element option and select sphere.

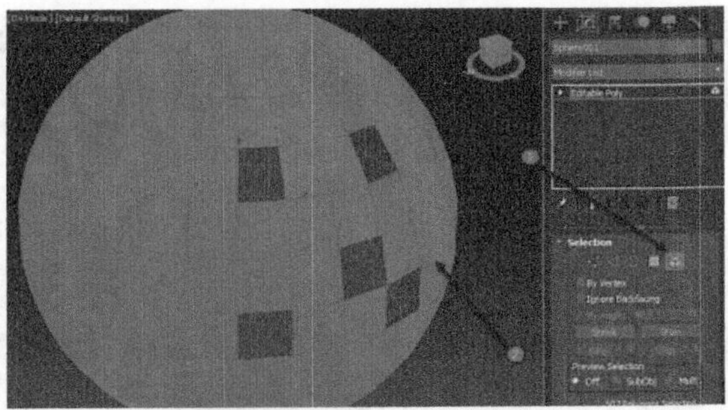

Figure 9 *Select element option*

Step 4: Click on modify tab and select cap holes tool.

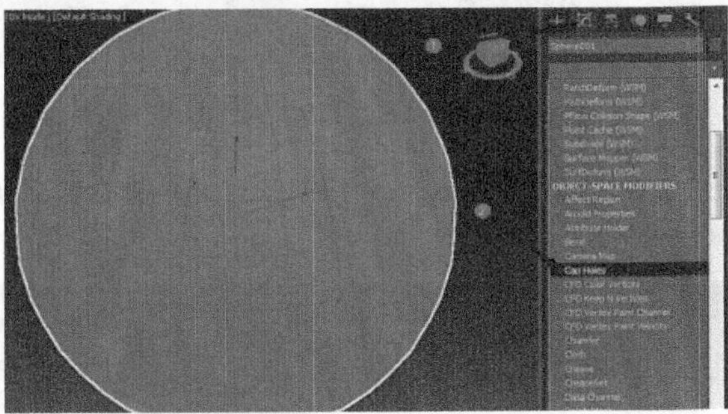

Figure 10 *Select cap holes tool*

CHAMFER

Chamfer tool is used to shape the curve to the edge of the object. With its help the edges can be smoothed.

Step 1: First of all, create a box.

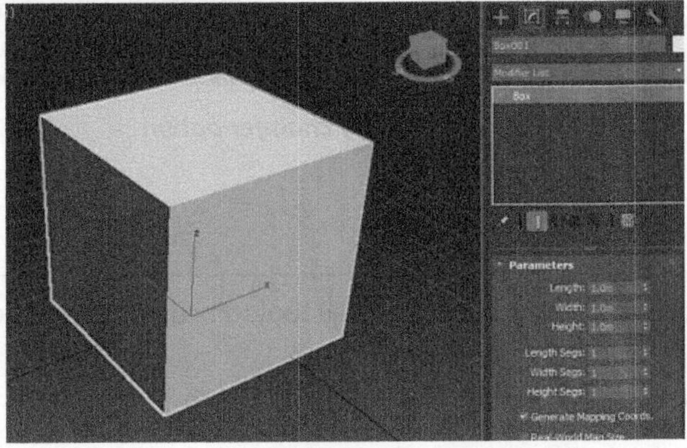

Figure 11 *Create a box*

Step 2: Select box and click on modify tab. Then click on chamfer tool.

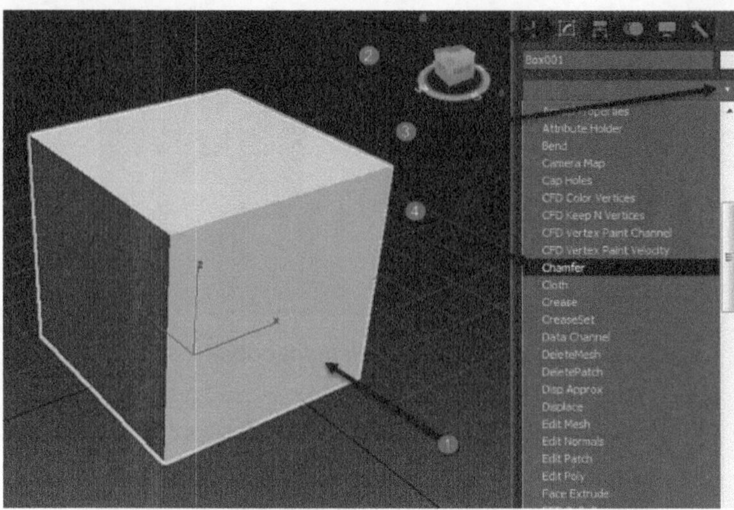

Figure 12 *Select chamfer tool*

Step 3: Select standard chamfer option in operation then set amount and segments.

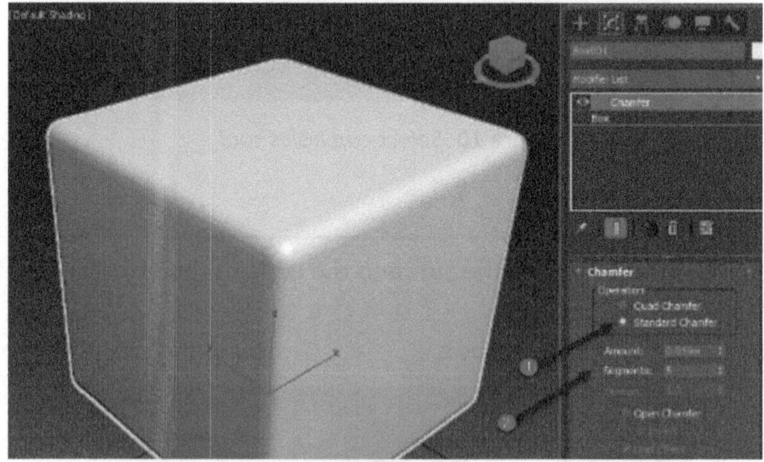

Figure 13 *Specify chamfer option*

CREASE

After shrinking objects, they use the crease tool to bring their vertices or edges back to their position.

Step 1: Create a box, then convert editable poly.

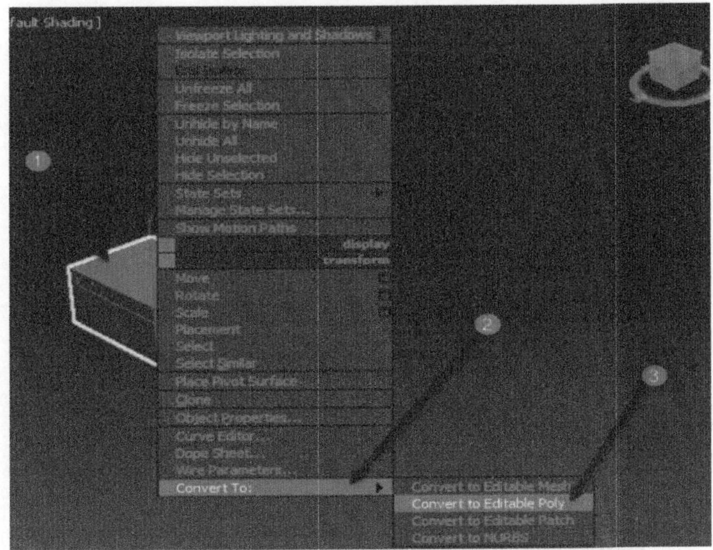

Figure 14 *Convert editable poly*

Step 2: Click on element option and select box.

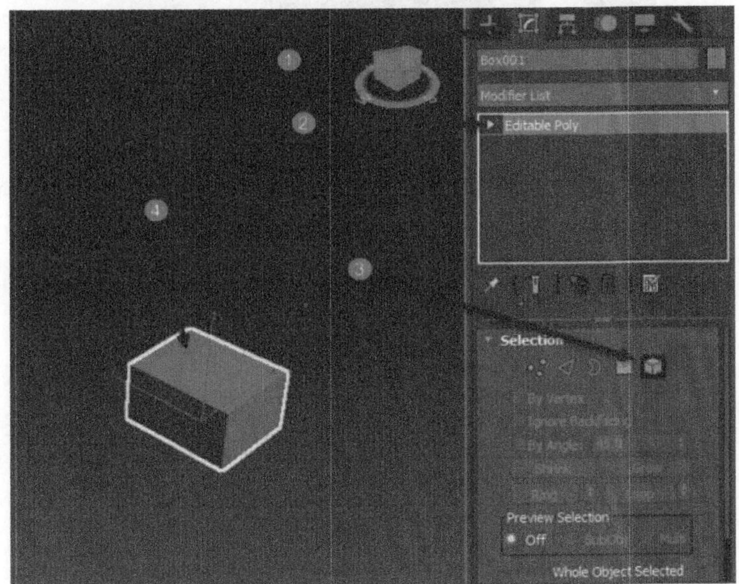

Figure 15 *Select element option*

Step 3: Click on modify tab and select crease tool.

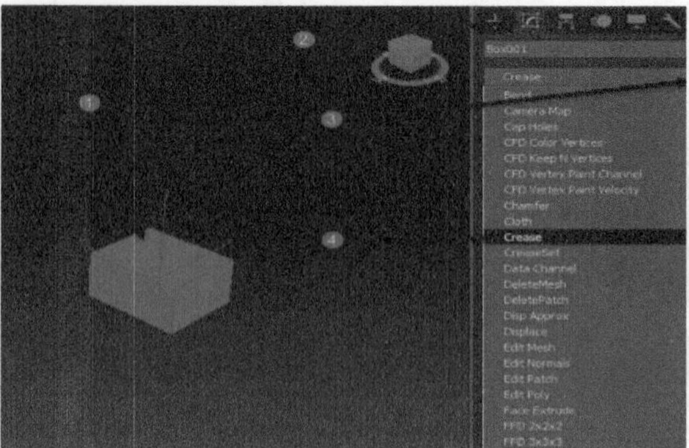

Figure 16 *Select crease tool*

Step 4: Again click on modify tab and select opensubdiv tool.

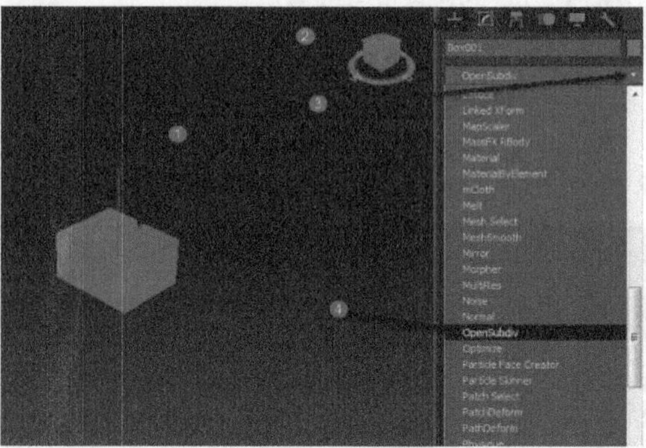

Figure 17 *Select opensubdiv tool*

Step 5: Select opensubdiv and specify iterations 2.

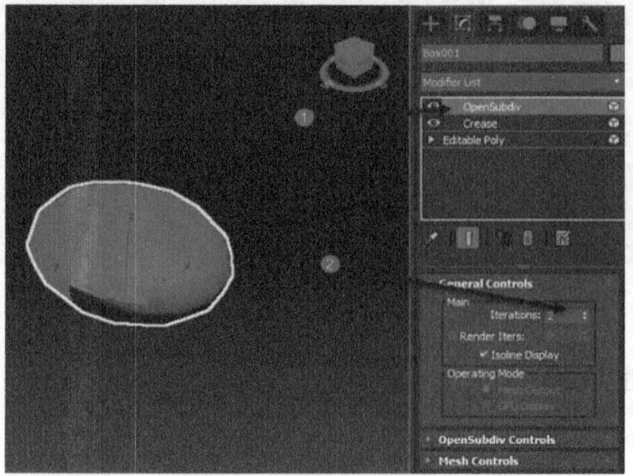

Figure 18 *Specify iterations*

Step 6: Select editable poly tool and select vertex option. Then select all vertex of box.

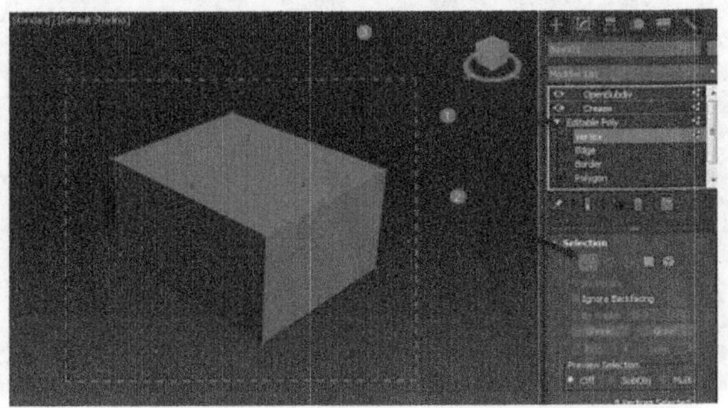

Figure 19 *Select editable poly and vertex option*

Step 7: After that select crease tool and specify crease value.

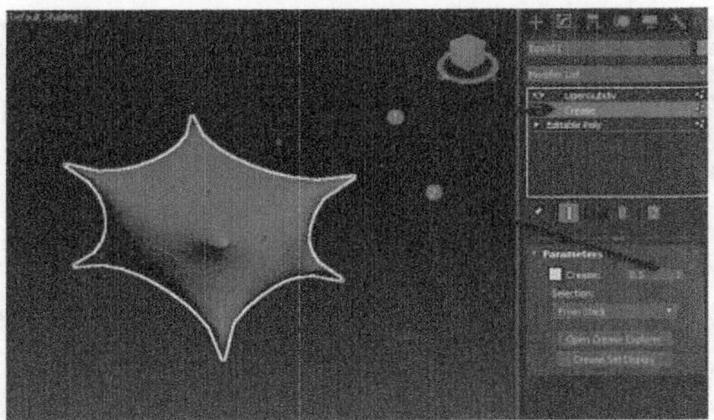

Figure 20 *Specify parameters of crease tool*

FACE EXTRUDE

The extrude modifier adds depth to a shape object and makes it a parametric object, and the Face Extrude modifier extrudes faces along their normals, creating new faces along the sides of the extrusion that connect the extruded faces to their object.

Step 1: Create a box and convert the box to editable poly.

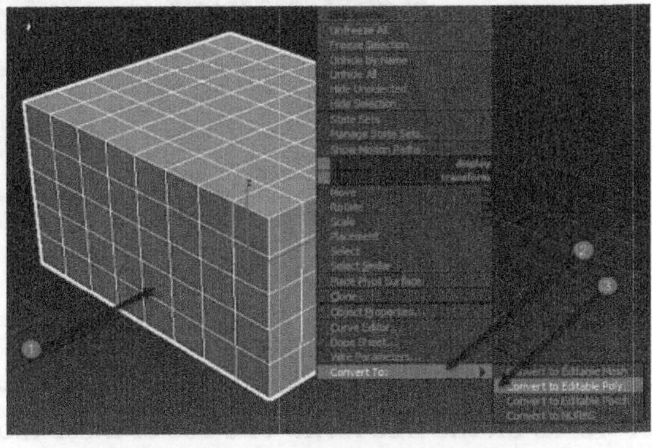

Figure 21 *Convert editable poly*

Step 2: Select polygon option of selection and select some faces of box.

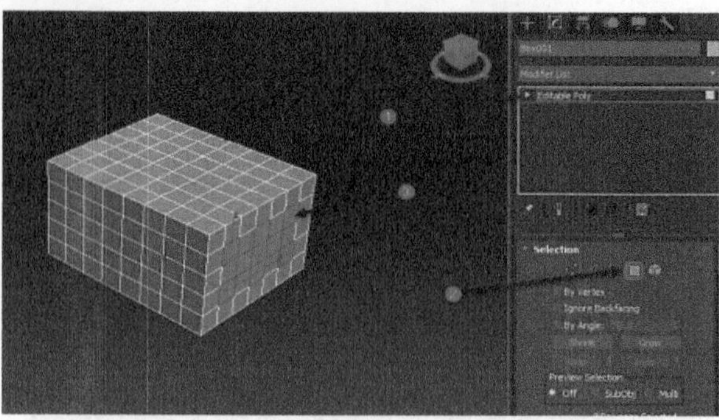

Figure 22 *Select face*

Step 3: After that click on modify tab and select face extrude tool.

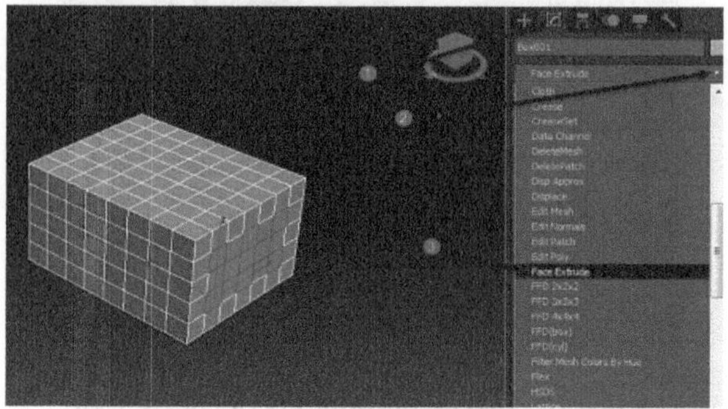

Figure 23 *Select face extrude tool*

Step 4: Specify extrude height.

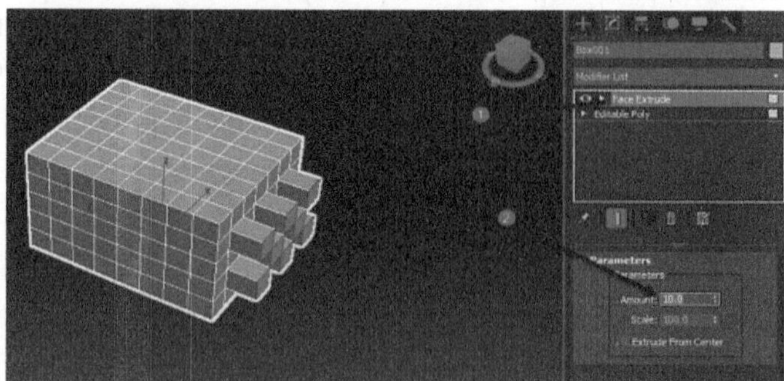

Figure 24 *Specify extrude height*

FFD 2X2X2

The FFD 2x2x2 tool works on the free form. The use of these tools is used to stretch the free model.

Step 1: Create a box and click modify tab then select FFD 2x2x2 tool.

Figure 25 *Use of ffd 2x2x2*

Step 2: Click on the flip arrow of the FFD 2x2x2 tool. Then select control point option.

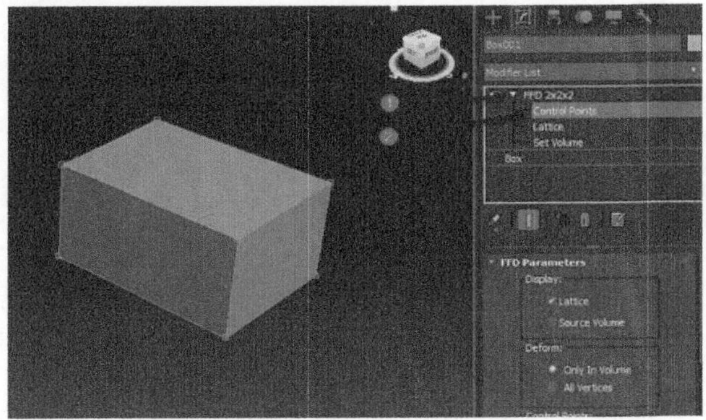

Figure 26 *Select control point option*

Step 3: Select move tool and select control point.

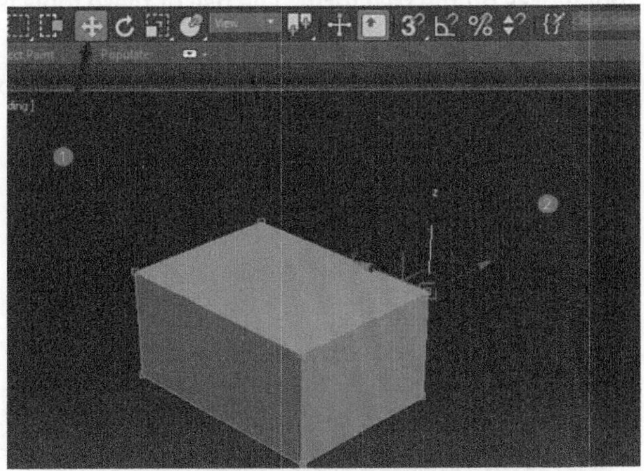

Figure 27 *Click on move tool*

Step 4: After that, click on Z-axis and drag up side.

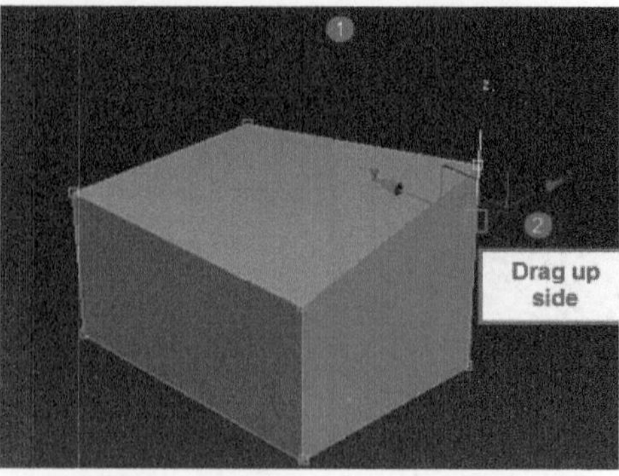

Figure 28 *Drag a control point*

These types of shapes can also be made from this tool.

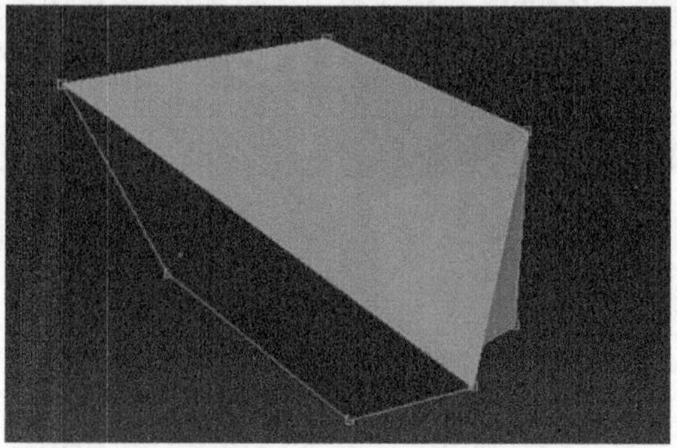

Figure 29 *Finale shape*

FFD 4X4X4

The FFD 4x4x4 tool works on the free form. The use of these tools is to to stretch the free model.

Step 1: Create a box and click modify tab then select FFD 4x4x4 tool.

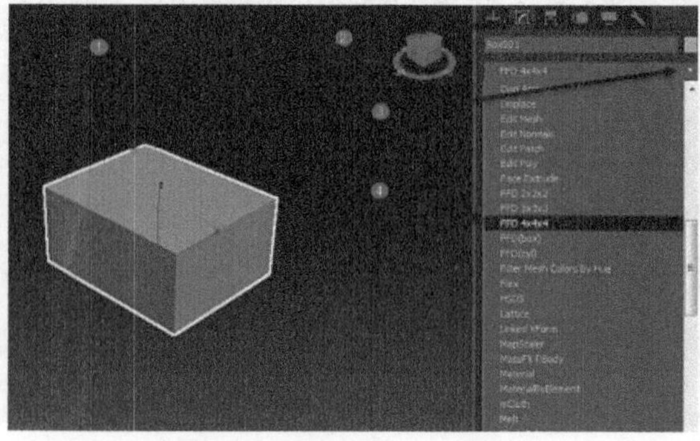

Figure 30 *Select ffd 4x4x4 tool*

Step 2: Click on the flip arrow of the FFD 4x4x4 tool. Then select control point option.

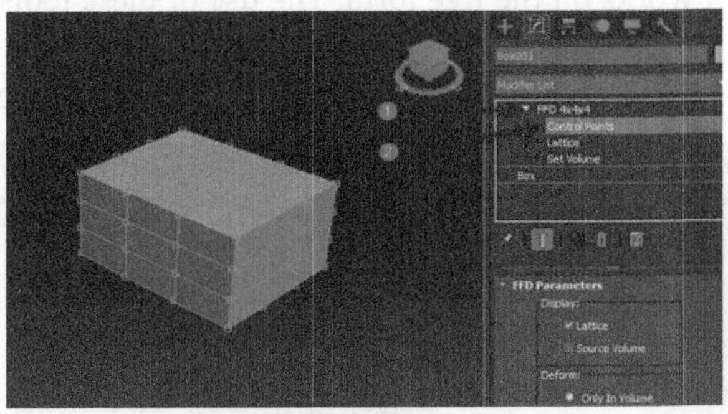

Figure 31 *Select control point option*

Step 3: Select scale tool and select some control point.

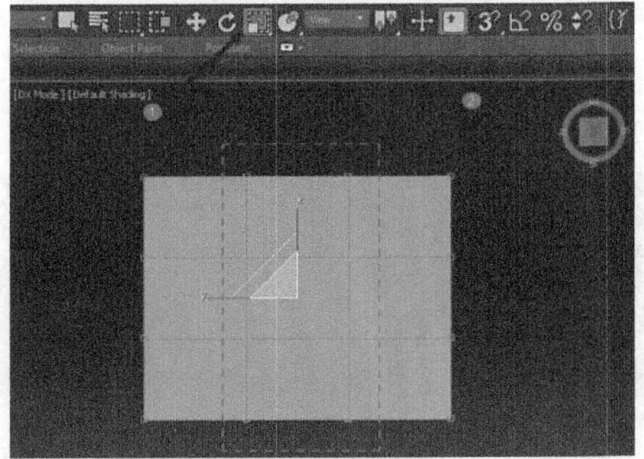

Figure 32 *Select scale tool*

Step 4: After that click on X-axis and drag up or down side.

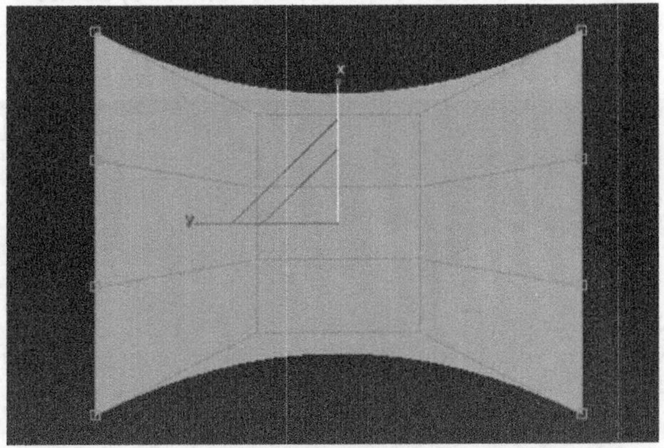

Figure 33 *Drag x axis*

FFD (BOX)

The FFD box tool works on the free form. The use of these tools is used to stretch the free model.

Step 1: Create a sphere and click modify tab then select FFD box tool.

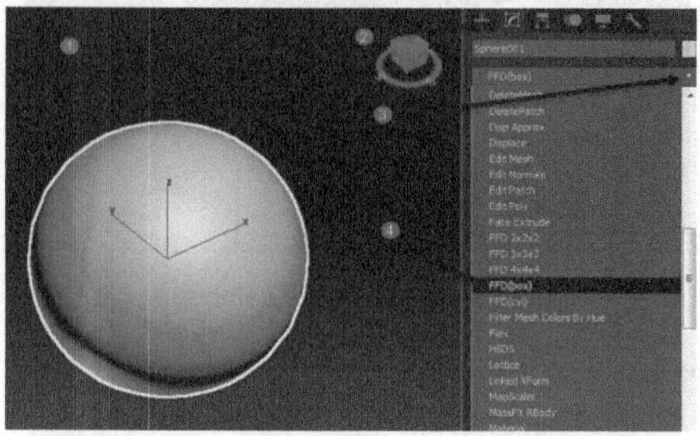

Figure 34 *Select ffd box tool*

Step 2: Click on button of set number.

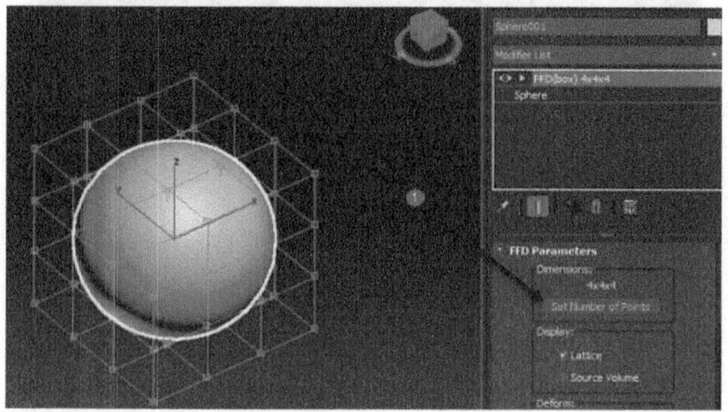

Figure 35 *Click on button of Set number of points*

Step 3: Set number of points.

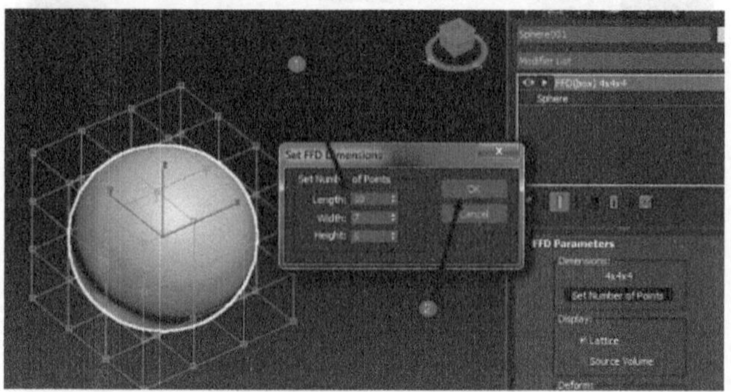

Figure 36 *Set ffd dimensions*

Step 4: Click on the flip arrow of the FFD box tool. Then select control point option.

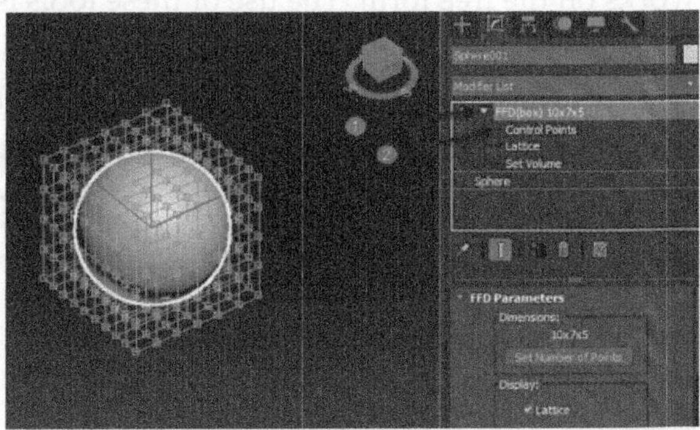

Figure 37 *Select control point option*

Step 5: Select move tool and select some control point.

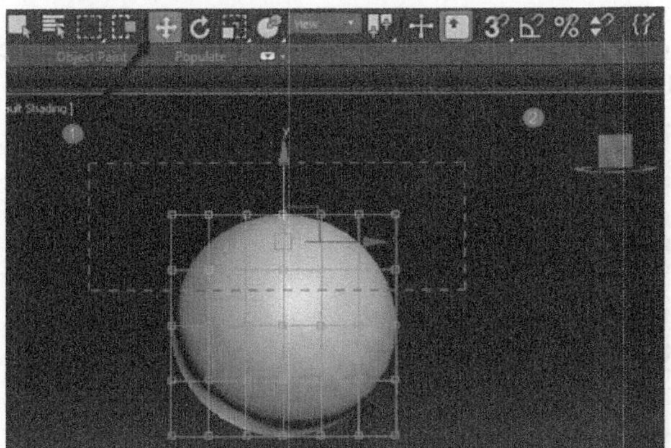

Figure 38 *Select move tool*

Step 6: Click on Y-axis and drag down side.

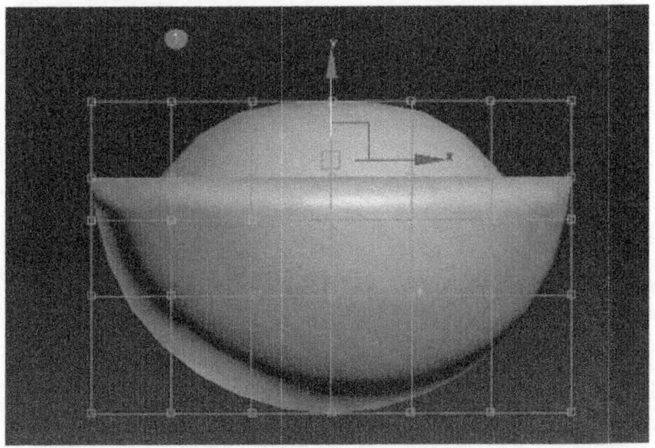

Figure 39 *Drag y axis*

FFD (CYL)

The FFD cyl tool works on the free form. The use of these tools is to stretch the free model.

Step 1: Create a sphere and click on modify tab then select FFD cyl tool.

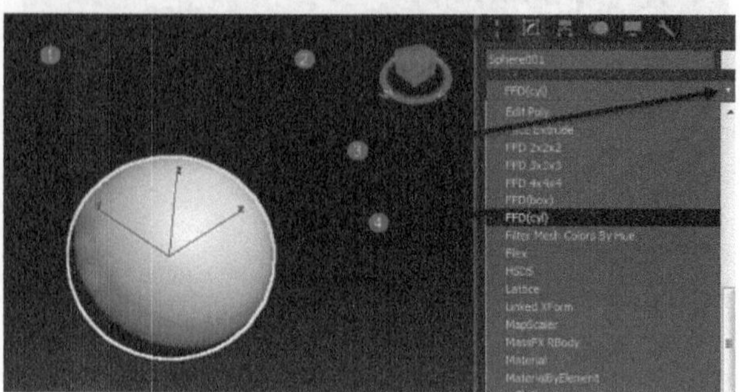

Figure 40 *Select FFD cyl tool*

Step 2: Click on the flip arrow of the FFD cyl tool. Then select control point option.

Figure 41 *Select control point option*

Step 3: Select scale tool and select some control point.

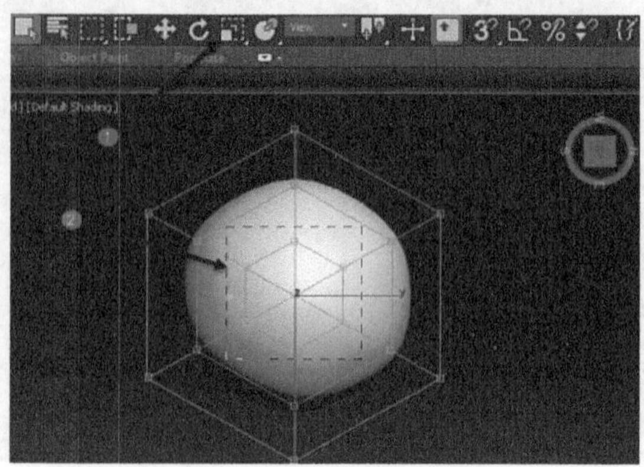

Figure 42 *Select scale tool*

Step 4: After that click on X-axis and drag up or down side.

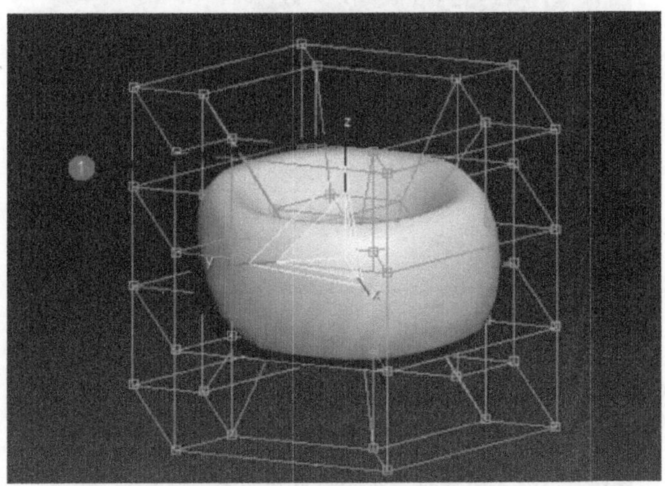

Figure 43 *Drag z axis*

HSDS

The HSDS modifier implements Hierarchical SubDivision Surfaces. It is intended primarily as a finishing tool rather than as a modeling tool. For best results, perform most of your modeling using low-polygon methods, and then use HSDS to add detail and adaptively refine the model.

Step 1: First of all, Create a cylinder then click on modify tab and select hsds tool.

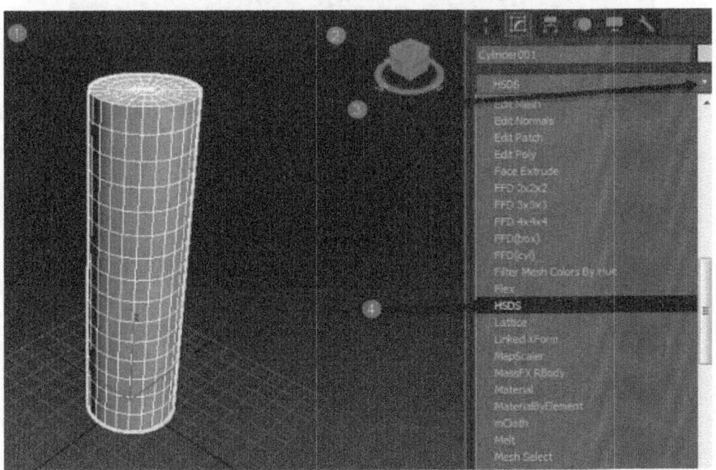

Figure 44 *Select hsds tool*

Step 2: Click on the edge option of hsds parametric.

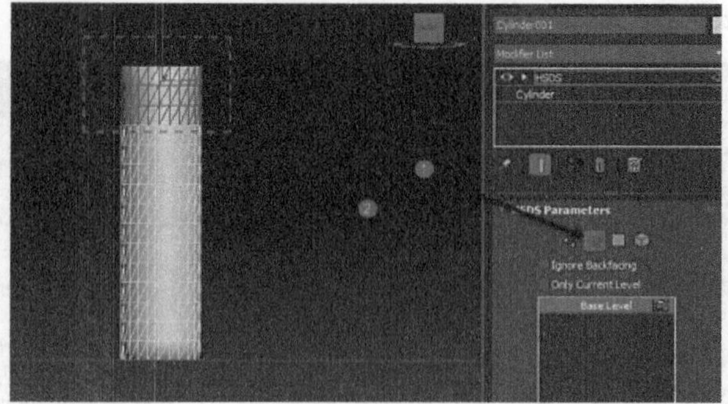

Figure 45 *Select edge option*

Step 3: Click on subdivide button.

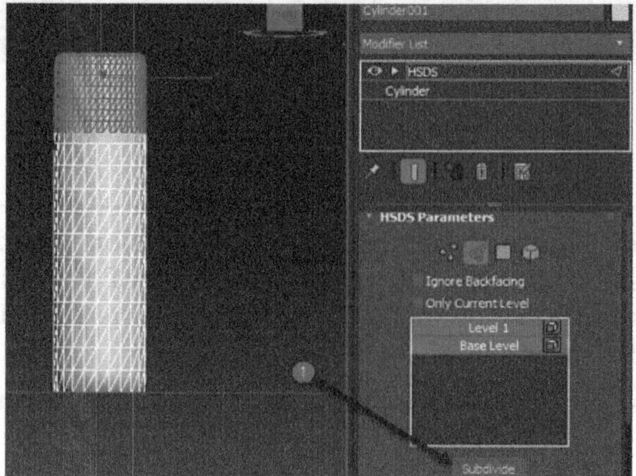

Figure 46 *Click on subdivide option*

Step 4: Click on move tool then again click on Z-axis and drag Z-axis.

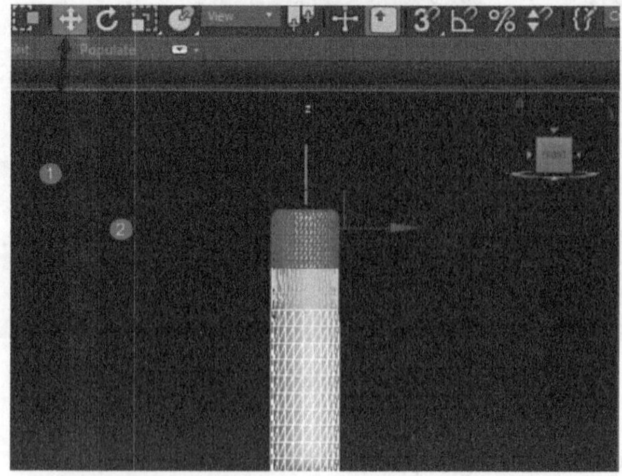

Figure 47 *Click on move tool and drag z axis*

Step 5: After that, click on scale tool then click on scale icon and drag down side.

Figure 48 *Click on scale tool and drag scale icon*

LATTICE

Use the Lattice tool to convert the model to wireframe shape. It can also give the thickness of the wire in it. They can also give different types of thickness.

Step 1: Create a box.

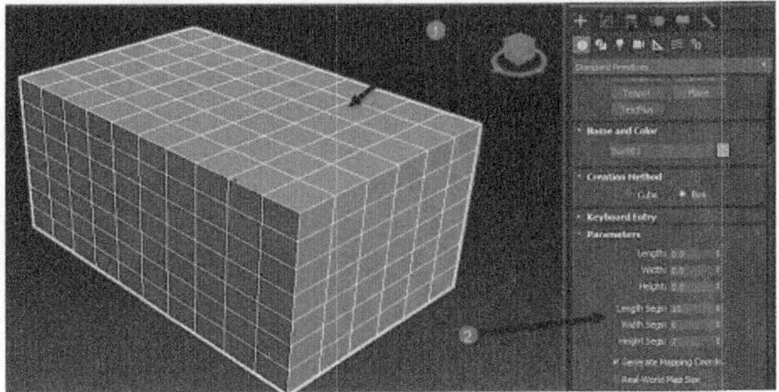

Figure 49 *Create a box*

Step 2: Select box then click on modify tab and select lattice tool.

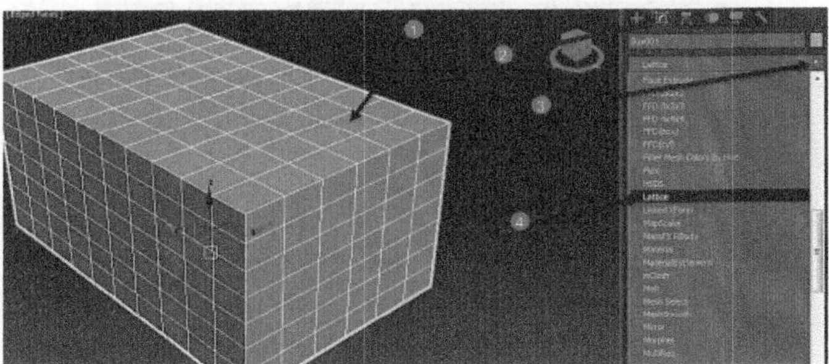

Figure 50 *Select lattice tool*

Step 3: After that specify radius, segments, and geodesic base type.

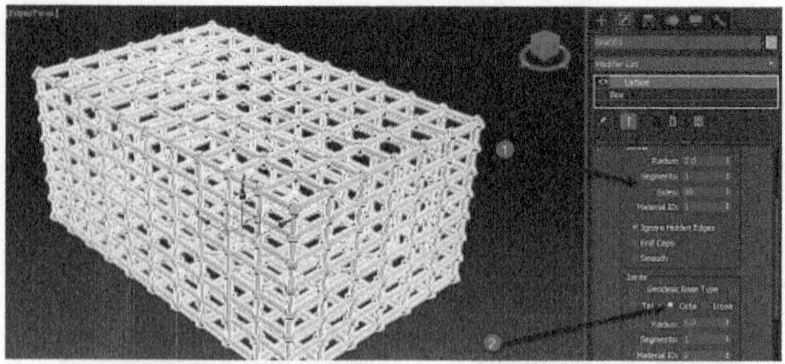

Figure 51 *Specify parametric of lattice tool*

MELT

The Melt modifier lets you apply a realistic melting effect to all types of objects, including editable patches and NURBS objects, as well as to sub-object selections passed up the stack. Use the Melt Tool to turn any shape into a melting shape. Such as ice, jelly, plastic, etc.

Step 1: First of all, create a sphere.

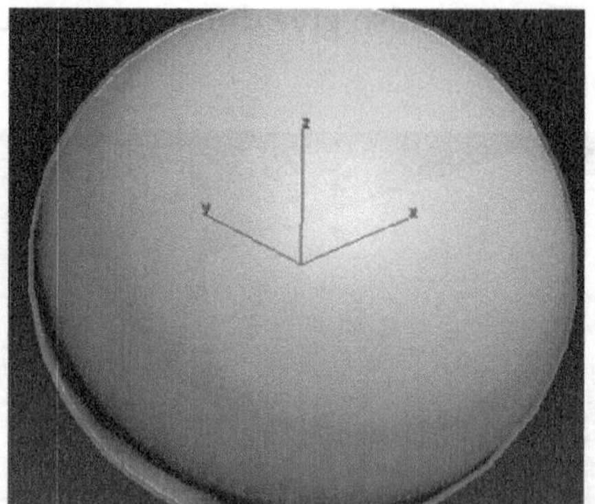

Figure 52 *Create a sphere*

Step 2: Click on modify tab and select melt tool.

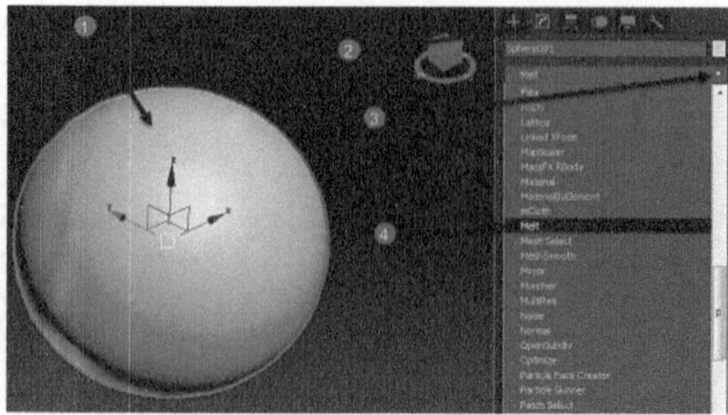

Figure 53 *Select melt tool*

Step 3: After that specify melt amount.

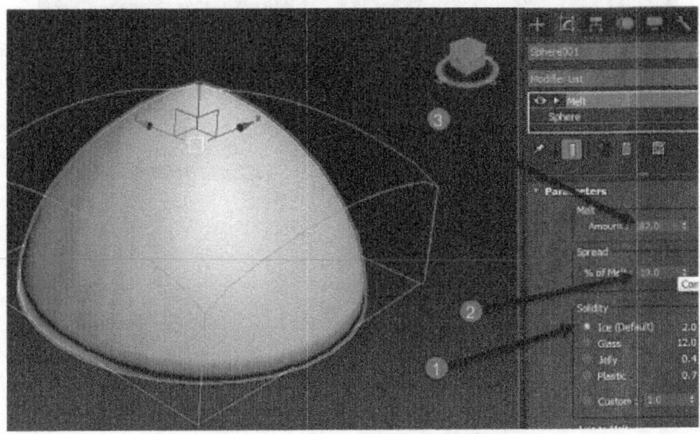

Figure 54 *Specify parameters*

MIRROR

The Mirror tool also allows you to mirror the current selection about the center of the current coordinate system. You can create a clone with the mirror dialog at the same time. If you want to mirror a hierarchical linkage, you have the option to mirror the IK limits. Use mirror tools to copy the inverse shape of the object.

Step 1: Create any object, as you want.

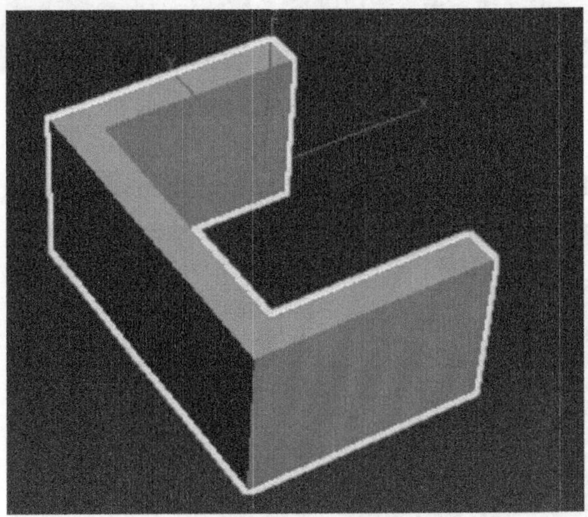

Figure 55 *Object*

Step 2: Click on modify tab and select mirror tool.

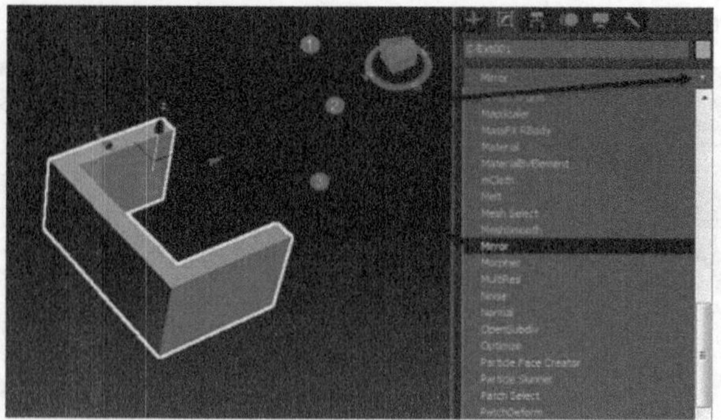

Figure 56 *Select mirror tool*

Step 3: Select mirror axis and copy option.

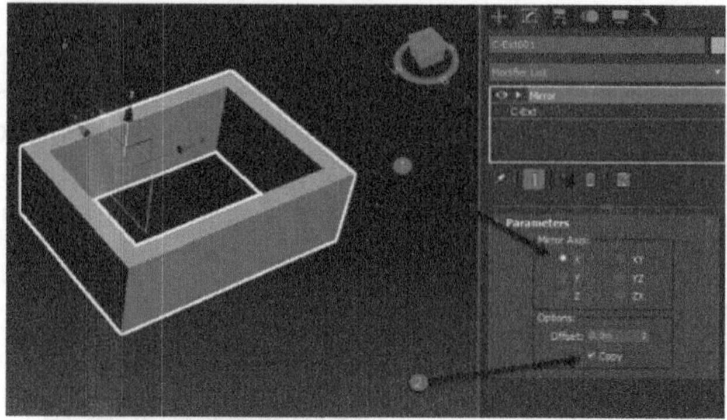

Figure 87 *Specify mirror axis*

Step 4: Click on flip arrow of mirror option then select mirror center option.

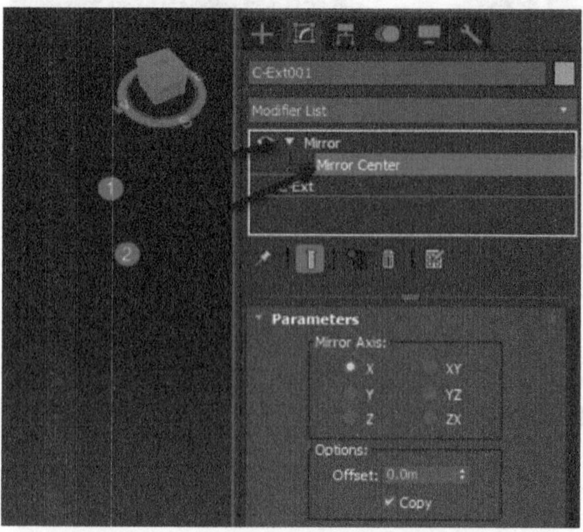

Figure 58 *Select mirror center option*

Step 5: After that, click on move tool then drag X-axis.

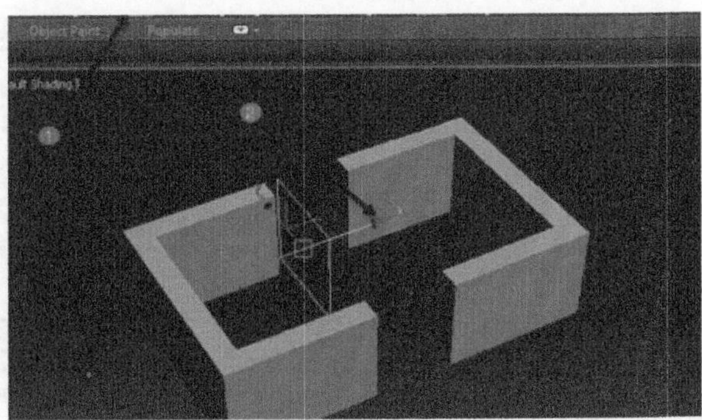

Figure 59 *Drag x axis*

STRETCH

Stretch tools are used to increase the pull of an object from any one side.

Step 1: Create a box.

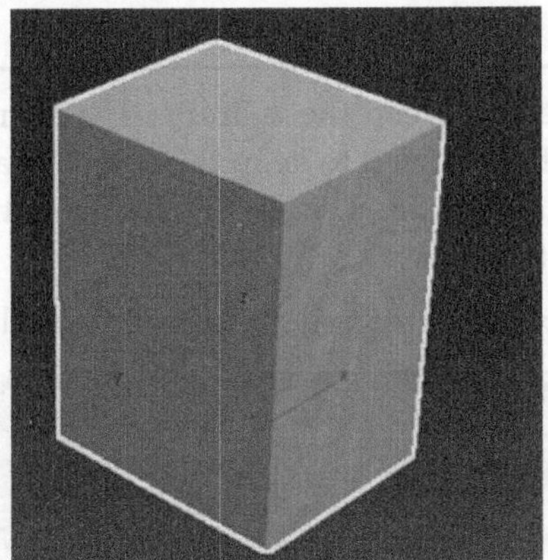

Figure 60 *Box*

Step 2: Click on modify tab and select stretch tool.

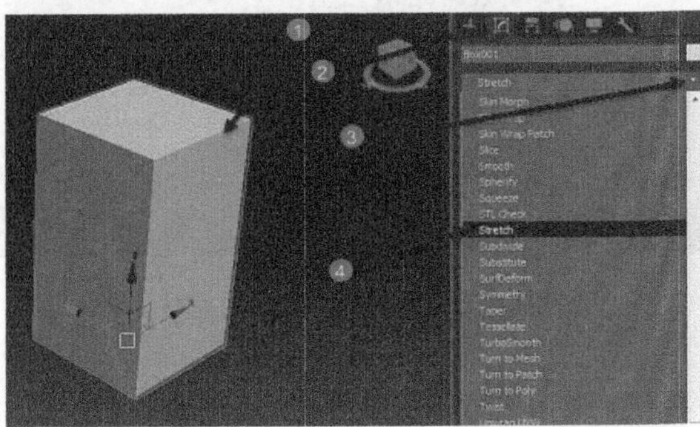

Figure 61 *Select stretch tool*

Step 3: Specify stretch parameters.

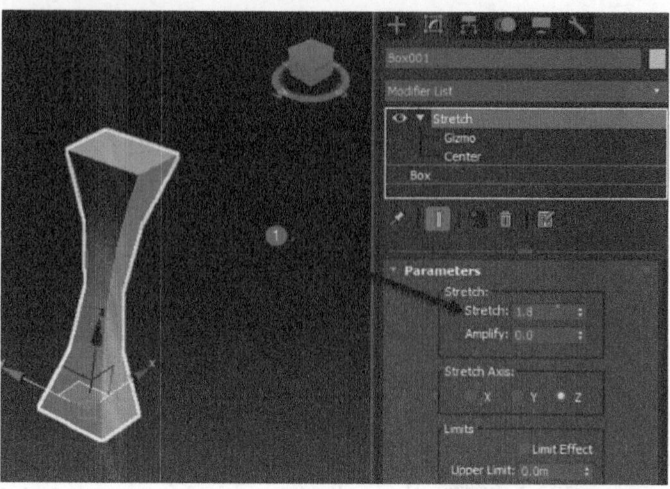

Figure 62 *Specify parameters*

TWIST

The twist offset is applied between these limits. The surrounding geometry, while unaffected by the twist itself, is moved to keep the object intact. At the sub-object level, you can select and move the modifier's center. The limit settings remain on either side of the center as you move it.

Step 1: Create a box and also give the segments of the box.

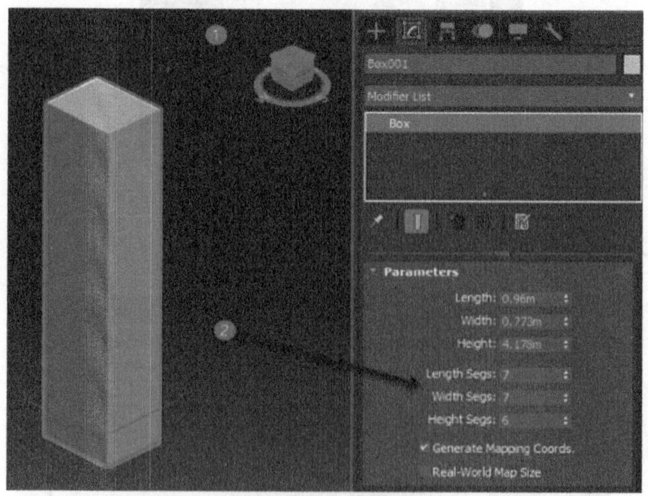

Figure 63 *Box with segments*

Step 2: Click on modify tab and select twist tool.

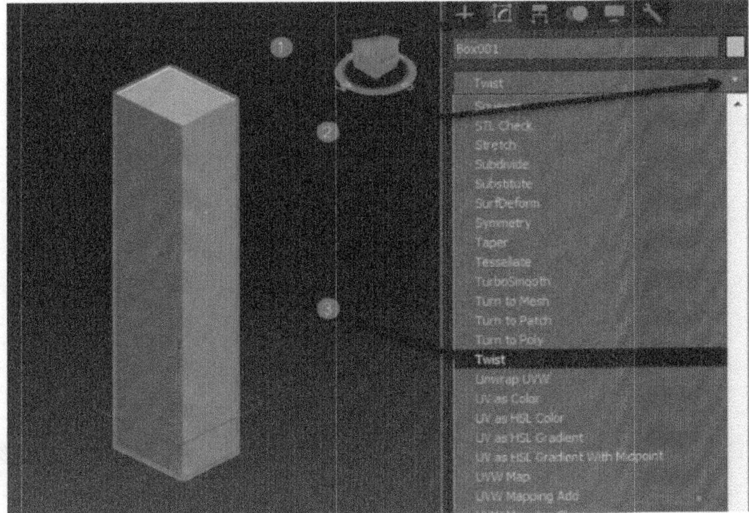

Figure 64 *Select twist tool*

Step 3: Specify twist angle and twist axis.

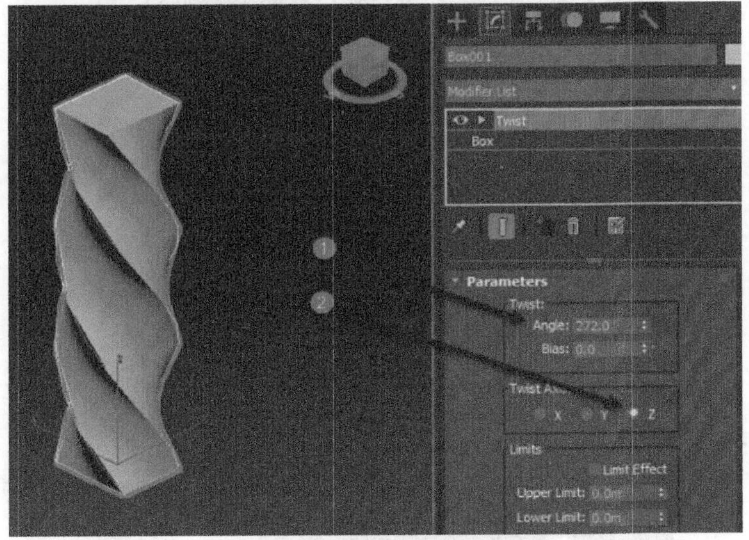

Figure 65 *Specify parameters*

MORPHER

If a tool has already been used with any other object, and that tool is now required to apply to any other object. Then use the morphar tool for it. Many tools can be applied together at this time.

Step 1: First of all, create a box with stretch tool.

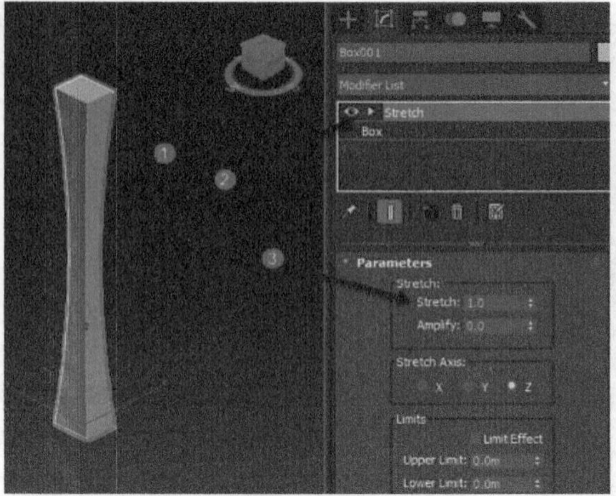

Figure 66 *Use stretch tool*

Step 2: After that, create a box with twist tool.

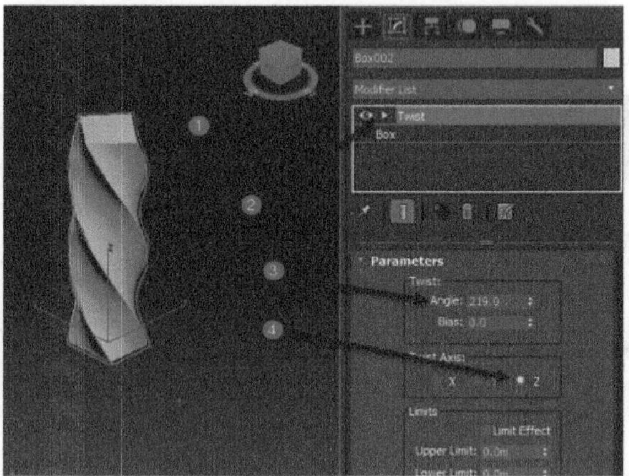

Figure 67 *Use twist tool*

Step 3: Now, again create a box for morpher.

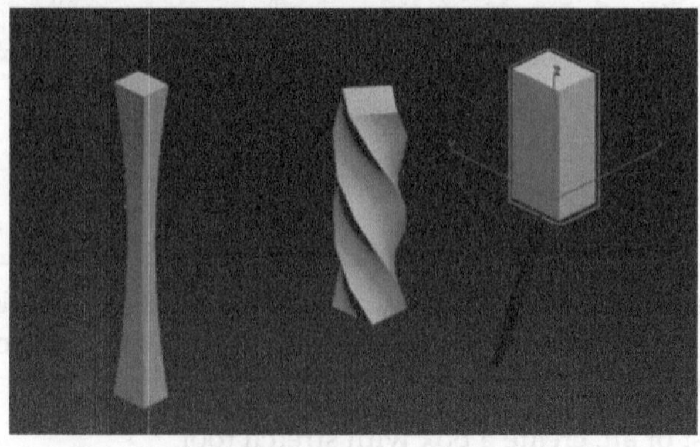

Figure 68 *Create 3rd box*

Step 4: Select the box which was made for the morpher. Then click on modify tab and select morpher tool.

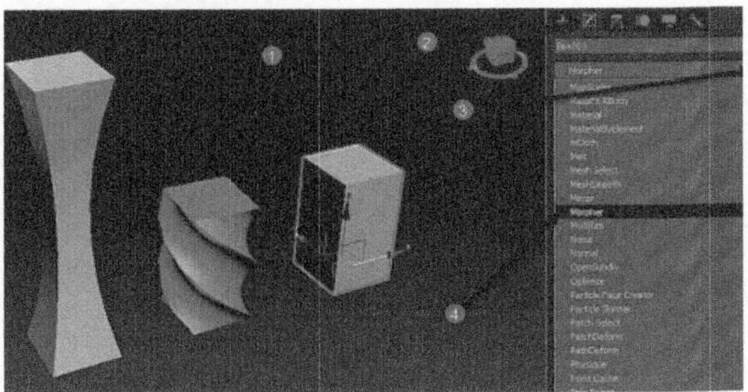

Figure 69 *Select morpher tool*

Step 5: Right click on empty button. Then click on pick from scene button.

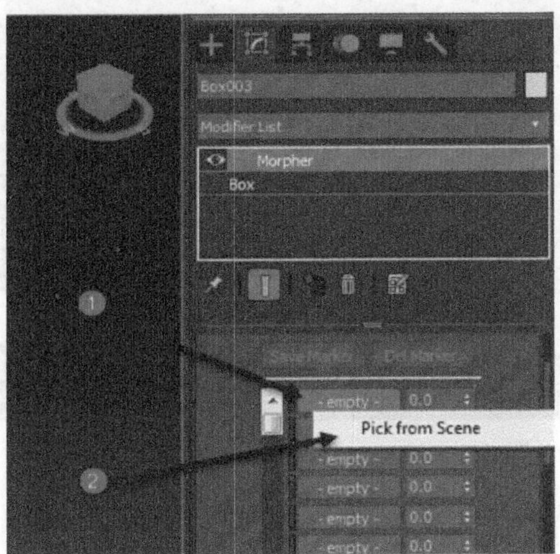

Figure 70 *Pick from scene*

Step 6: Then pick first box that was stretch.

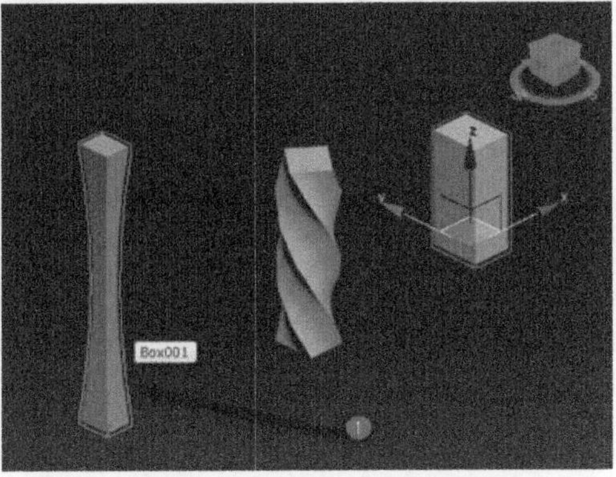

Figure 71 *Pick stretch box*

Step 7: Again right click on empty button. However, on second button. Then click on pick from scene button.

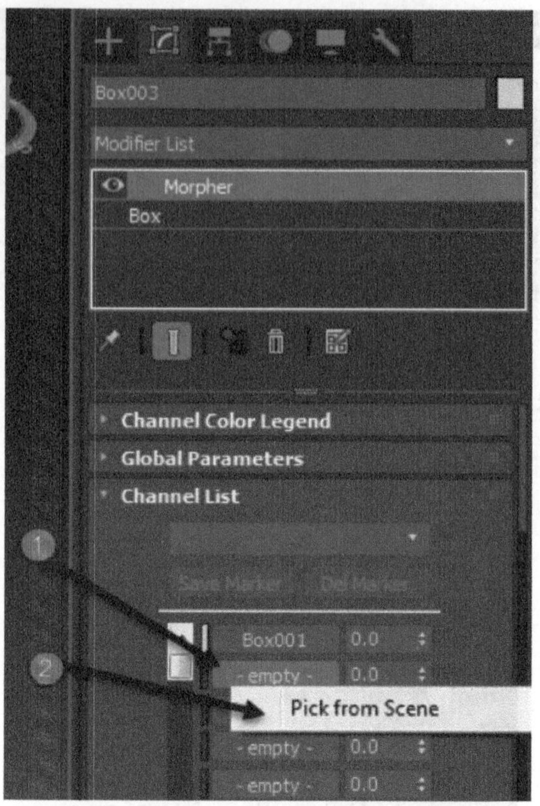

Figure 72 *Pick from scene*

Step 8: Then pick second box that was twist.

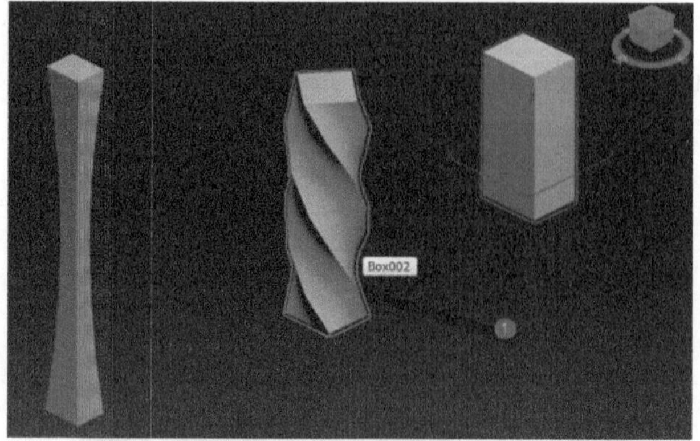

Figure 73 *Pick twist box*

Step 9: After that, specify value of stretch and twist.

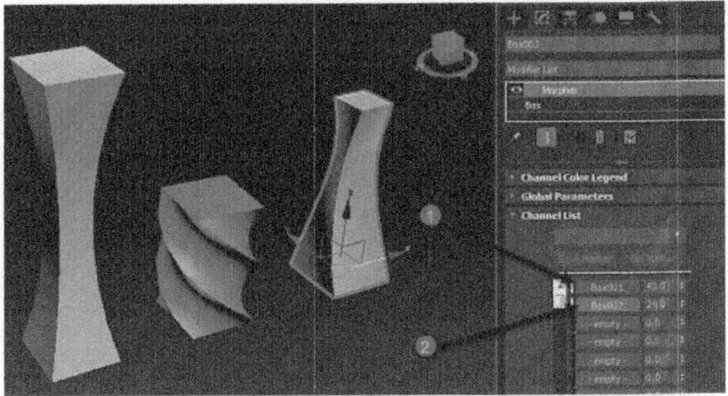

Figure 74 *Specify value*

NOISE

When set for fractal, the Noise modifier produces a random fractal noise that creates a variety of topological and terrain effects. In the Parameters rollout Noise group, turn on Fractal. Roughness and Iterations settings are now available. Increase strength on the Z-axis and adjust other parameters.

Step 1: First of all, create a plane.

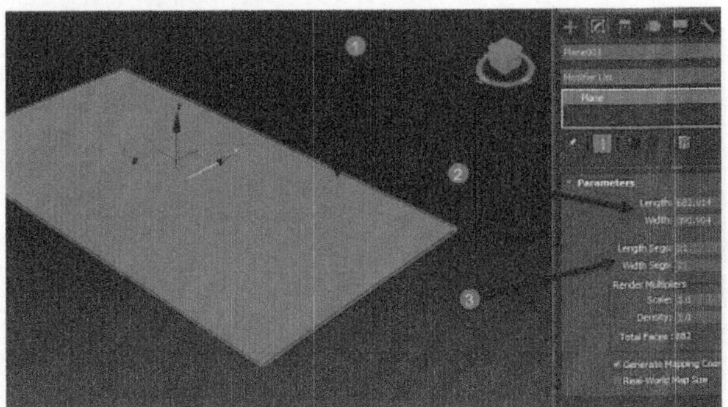

Figure 75 *Plane*

Step 2: Click on modify tab then select noise tool.

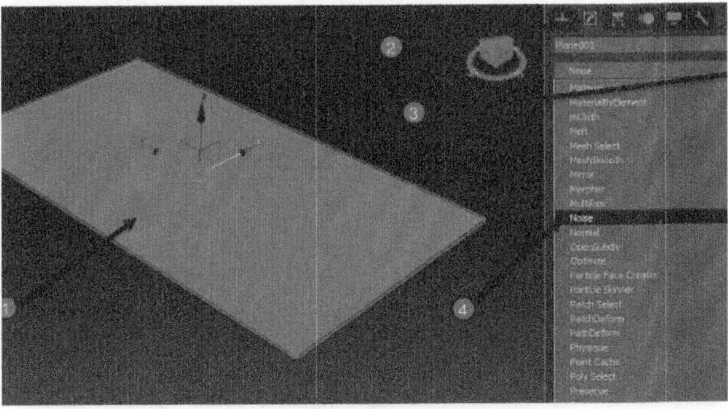

Figure 76 *Select noise tool*

Step 3: After that, specify parameters.

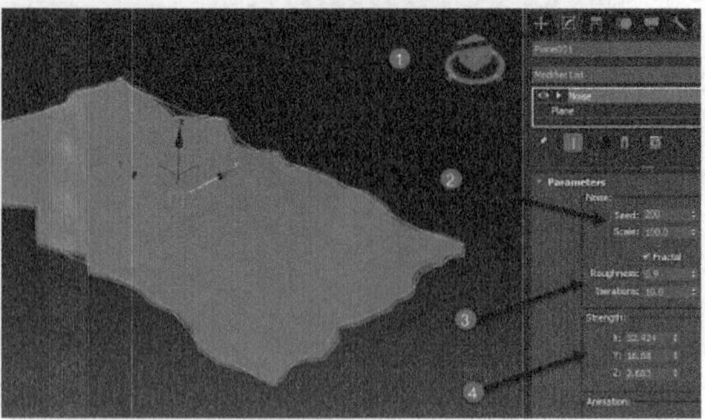

Figure 77 *Specify parameters*

OPENSUBDIV

The OpenSubdiv modifier performs subdivision and smoothing of mesh objects. It also reads Crease values from underlying stack entries and applies them to the modified object.

Step 1: Create a box.

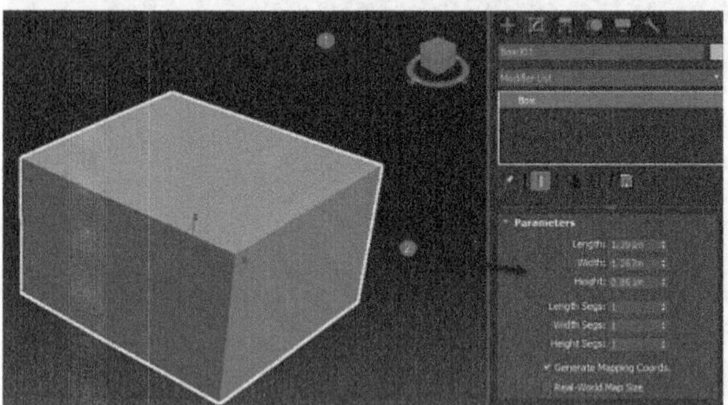

Figure 78 *Box*

Step 2: Click on modify tab then select opensudiv tool.

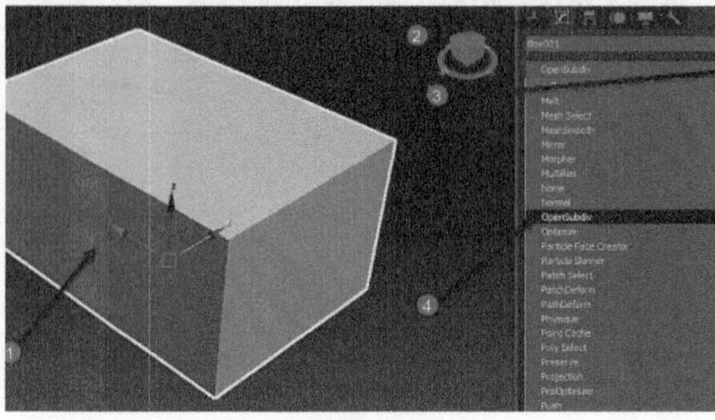

Figure 79 *Select opensubdiv tool*

Step 3: Specify iterations.

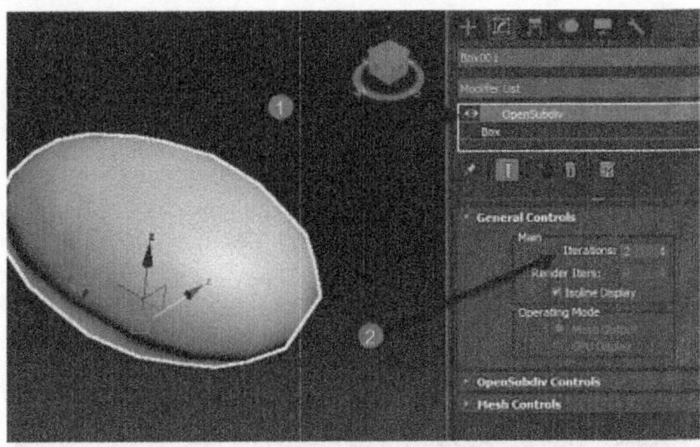

Figure 80 *Specify iterations value*

OPTIMIZE

The Optimize modifier lets you reduce the number of faces and vertices in an object. This simplifies the geometry and speeds up rendering while maintaining an acceptable image. A before/after readout gives you exact feedback on the reduction as you make each change.

Step 1: First of all, create a teapot.

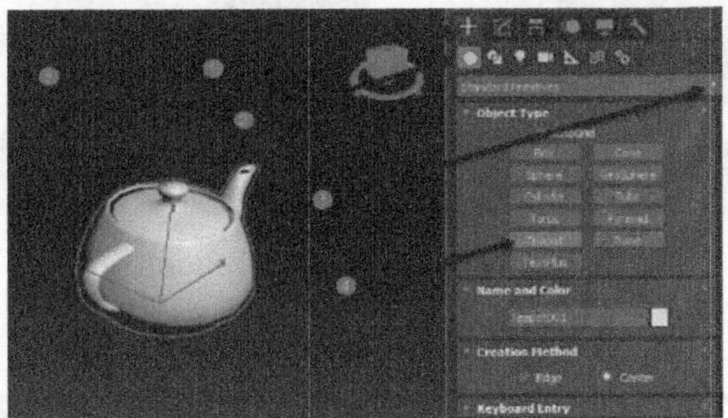

Figure 81 *teapot*

Step 2: Click on Move tool and select **Teapot**. Then press shift key and drag Z-axis.

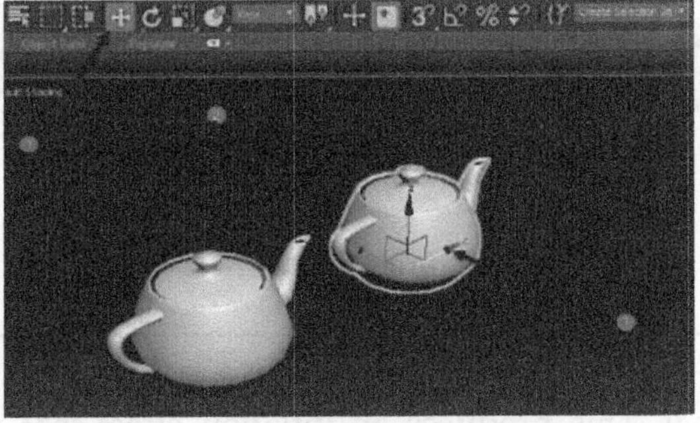

Figure 82 *Copy from move tool*

Step 3: Select number of copy and click on **OK**.

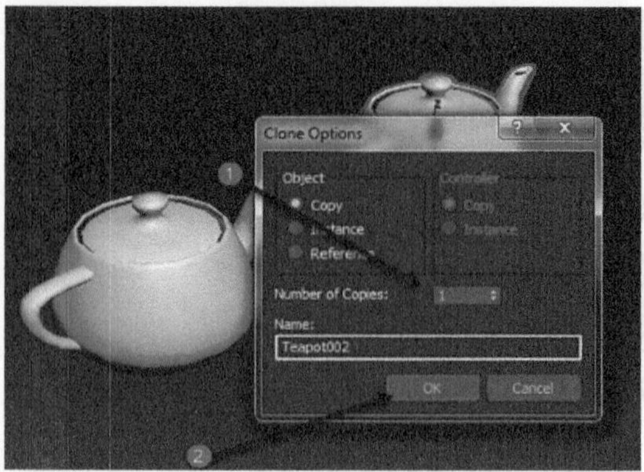

Figure 83 *Set number of copies*

Step 4: Select second teapot, then click on modify tab and select optimize tool.

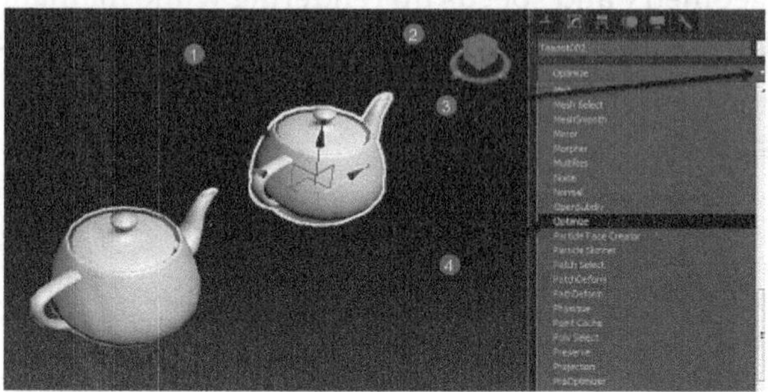

Figure 84 *Select optimize tool*

Step 5: After that, specify parameters.

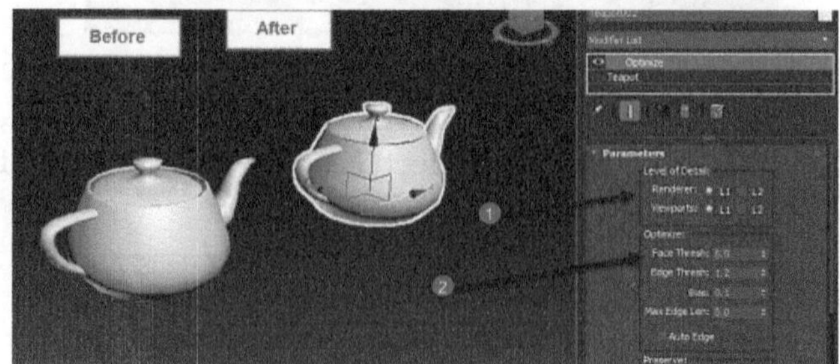

Figure 85 *Specify parameters*

PUSH

The Push modifier lets you push object vertices outward or inward along the average vertex normal. This produces an inflation effect that you can't otherwise obtain. Positive and negative amounts of push applied to an object.

Step 1: Create a teapot.

Figure 86 *Teapot*

Step 2: Click on modify tab and select push tool.

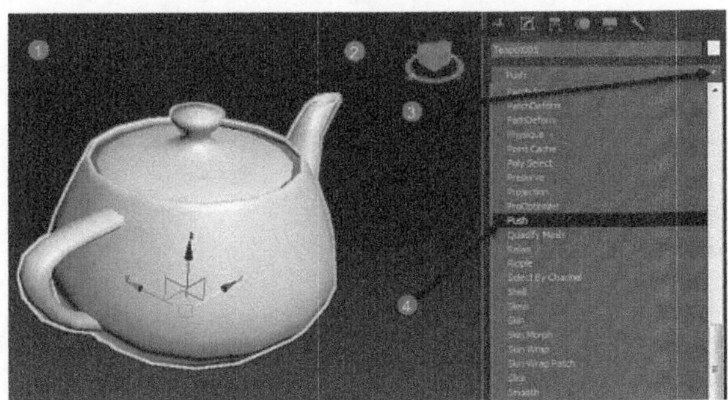

Figure 87 *Select push tool*

Step 3: Specify push value.

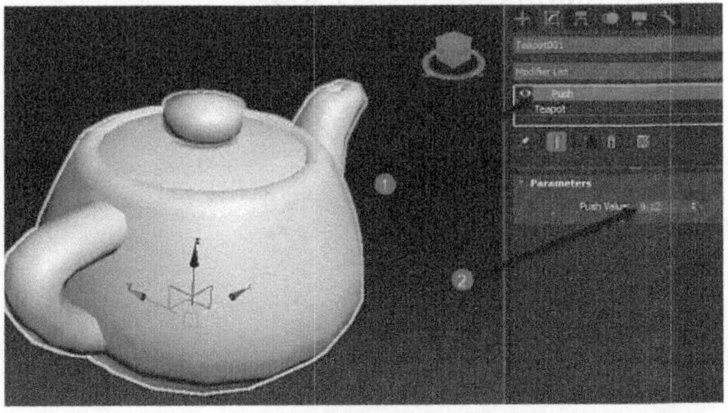

Figure 88 *Specify push value*

RIPPLE

The Ripple modifier produces a concentric rippling effect in an object's geometry. You can use either of the two different ripple effects or a combination of both. Ripple uses a standard gizmo and center, which you can transform to increase the number of ripple variations. The Ripple space warp has similar features.

Step 1: Create a plane.

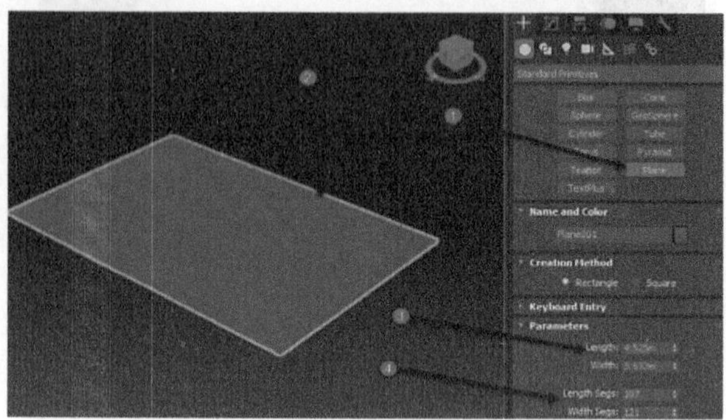

Figure 89 *Plane*

Step 2: Click on modify tab then select Ripple tool.

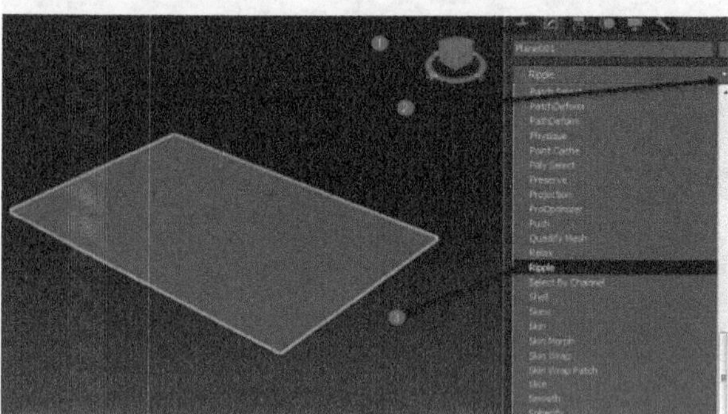

Figure 90 *Select ripple tool*

Step 3: Specify amplitude and wave length.

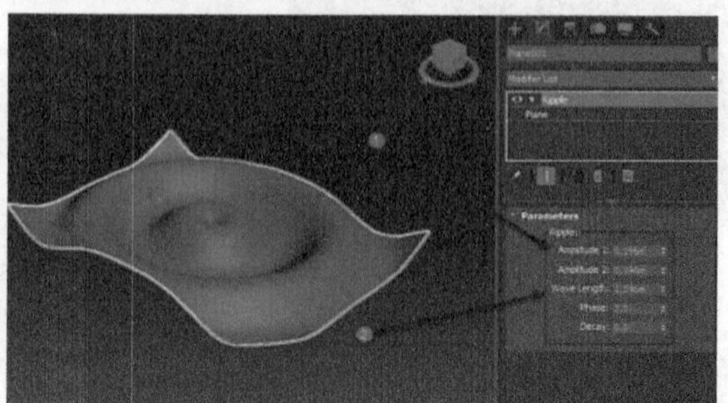

Figure 91 *Specify parameters*

SHELL

Welcome to studio pixel, this tutorial is all about the shell modifier in 3ds max now. Shell modifier is a very exclusive modifier which actually helps you to give the thickness of your surface.

Step 1: Create a box with one segment.

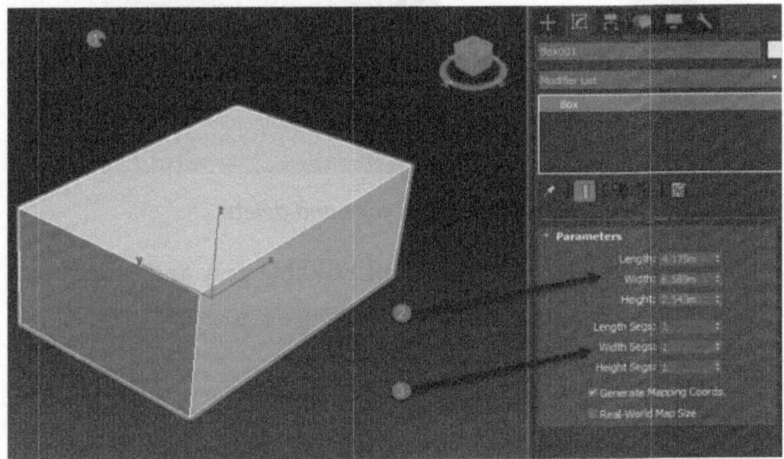

Figure 92 *Box*

Step 2: Convert box to editable poly by right clicking on the box.

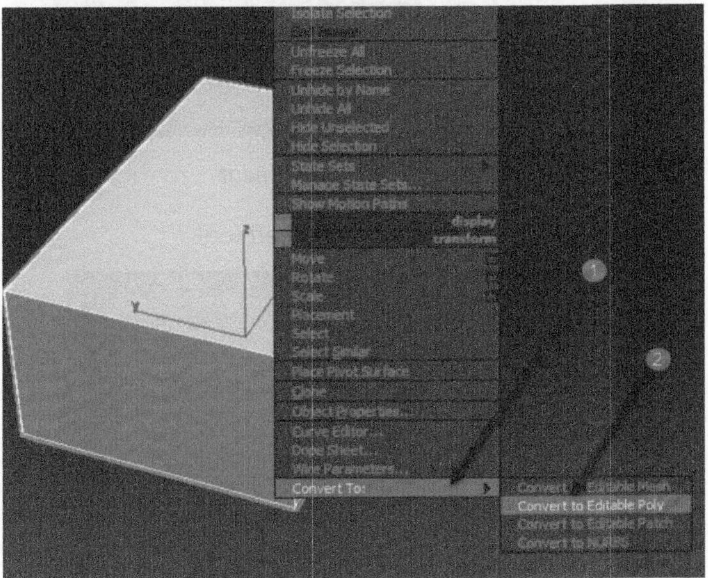

Figure 93 *Convert to editable poly*

Step 3: Click on the Polygon option of Editable poly. Then select face of the box and delete.

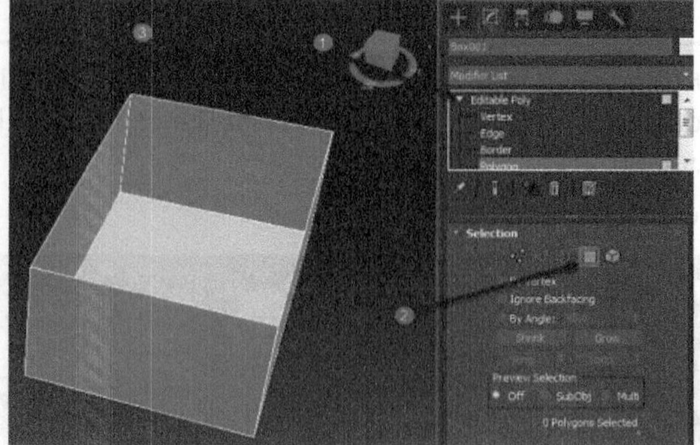

Figure 94 *Select face and delete*

Step 4: Click on the element option of Editable poly and select box.

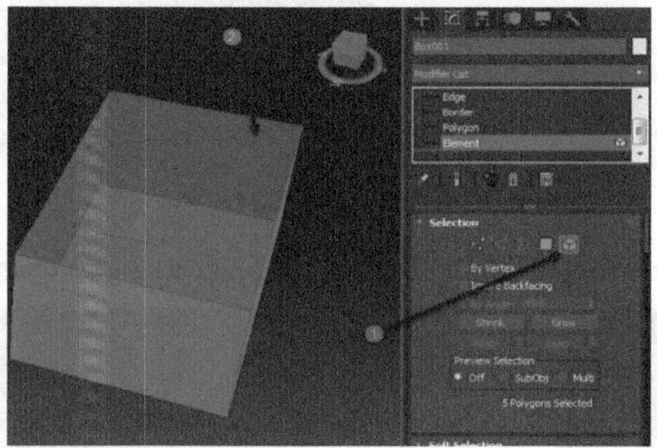

Figure 95 *Select element*

Step 5: Click on modify tab then select Shell tool.

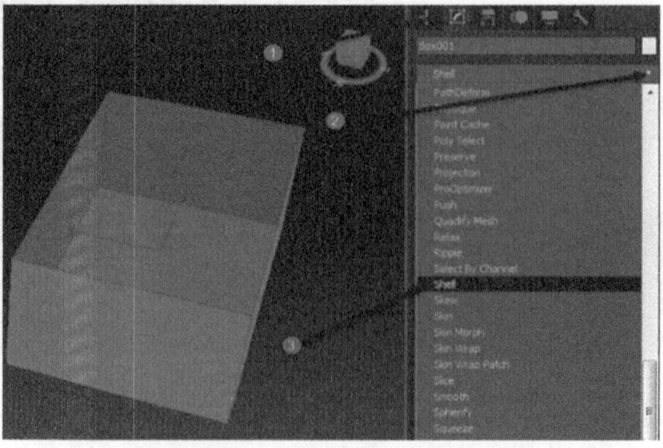

Figure 96 *Select shell tool*

Step 6: Specify parameters.

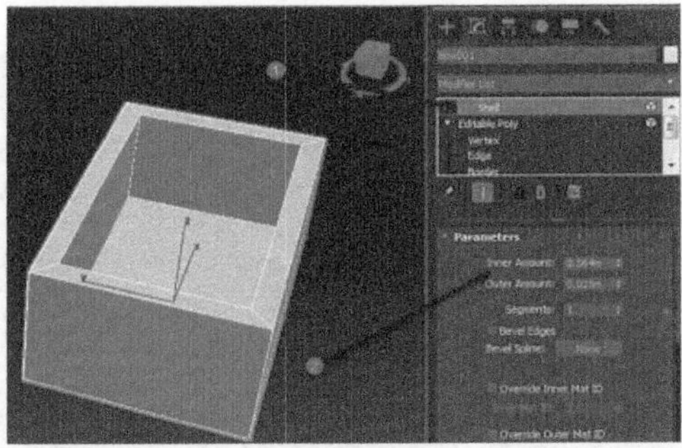

Figure 97 *Specify parameters*

RELAX

The Relax modifier changes the apparent surface tension in a mesh by moving vertices closer to, or away from, their neighbors. The typical result is that, the object gets smoother and a little smaller as the vertices move toward an average center point. You can see the most pronounced effects on objects with sharp corners and edges.

Step 1: Create a plane.

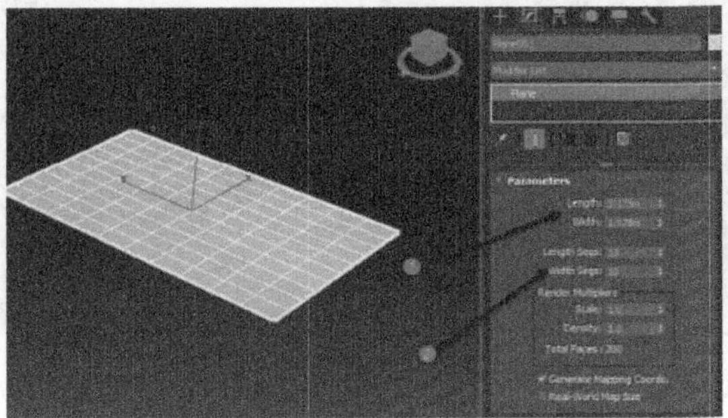

Figure 98 *Plane*

Step 2: Convert plan to editable poly by right clicking on the plan.

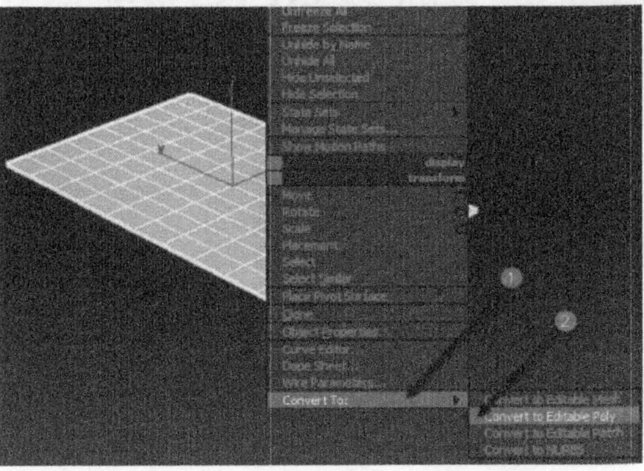

Figure 99 *Convert to editable poly*

Step 3: Click on the Vertex option of Editable poly. Then select two vertex of plan.

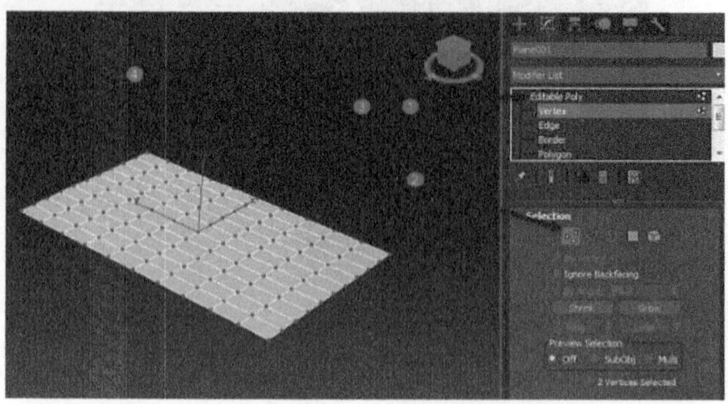

Figure 100 *Select vertex*

Step 4: Right click on the move tool. Then specify distance of Z-axis.

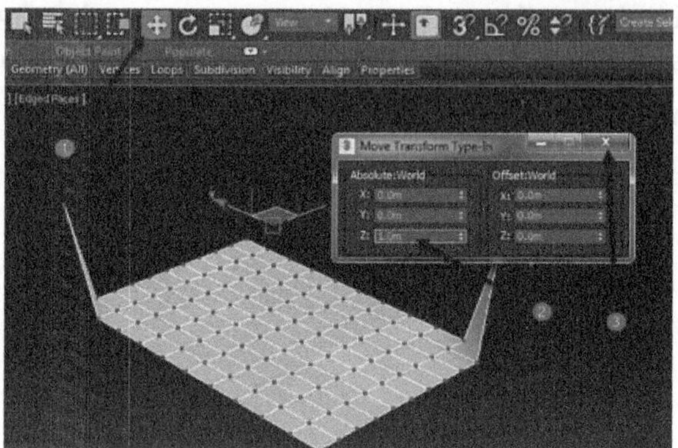

Figure 101 *Select move tool and specify z axis distance*

Step 5: Select all the vertex then click on modify tab and select relax tool.

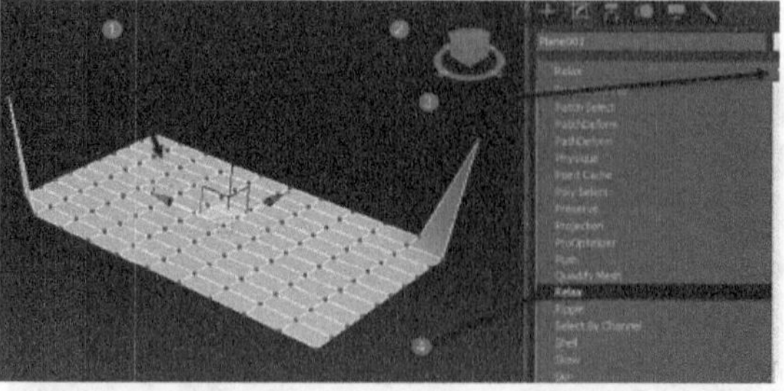

Figure 102 *Select relax tool*

Step 6: First uncheck keep boundary pts fixed option and specify parameters.

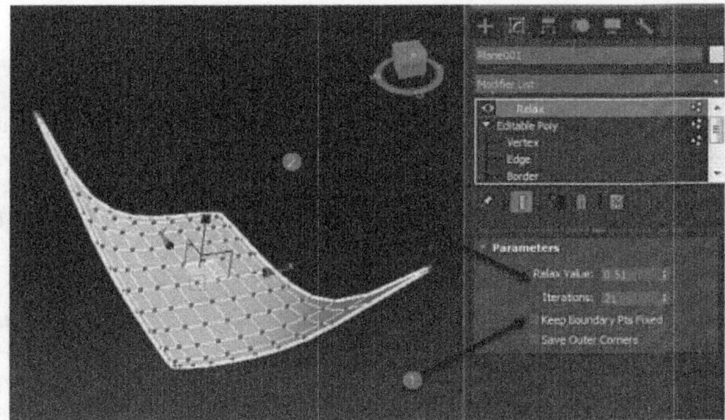

Figure 103 *Set parameters*

SKEW

The Skew modifier let you produce a uniform offset in an object's geometry. You can control the amount and direction of the skew on any of three axes. You can also limit the skew to a section of the geometry.

Step 1: Create a box.

Figure 104 *Box*

Step 2: Click on modify tab and select skew tool.

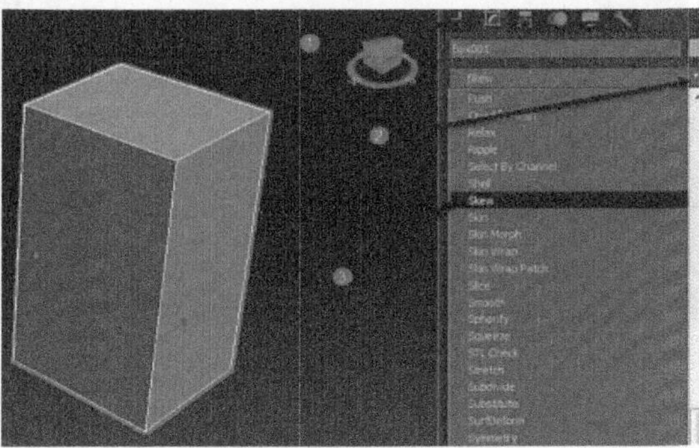

Figure 105 *Select skew tool*

Step 3: Set Z-axis and specify skew amount.

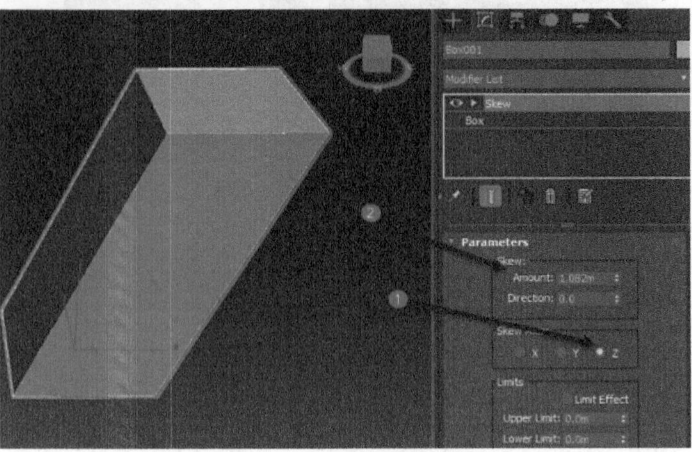

Figure 106 *Specify parameters*

SLICE

The Slice modifier lets you use a cutting plane to slice through a mesh, creating new vertices, edges, and faces based on the location of the slice plane gizmo. The vertices can either refine (subdivide) or split the mesh, and you can also remove the mesh from one side of the plane.

Step 1: Create a sphere.

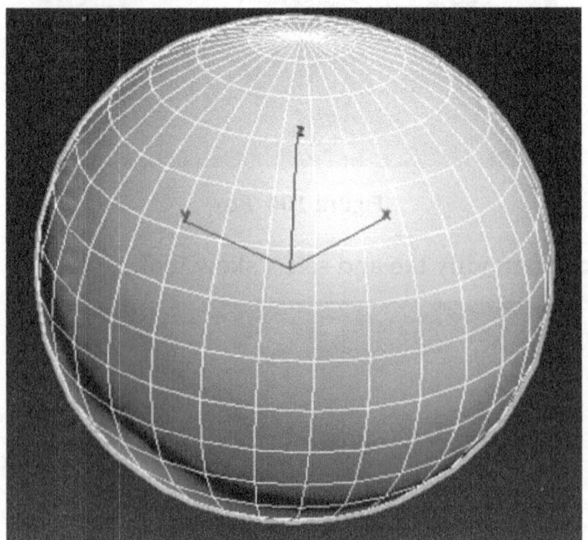

Figure 107 *Sphere*

Step 2: Click on modify tab and select slice tool.

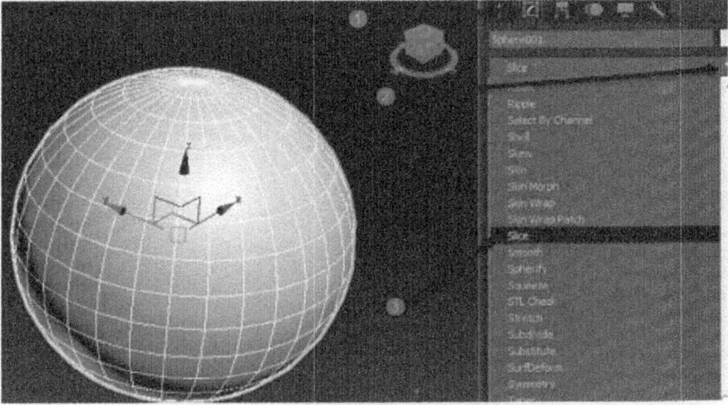

Figure 108 *Select slice tool*

Step 3: Click on remove top option button.

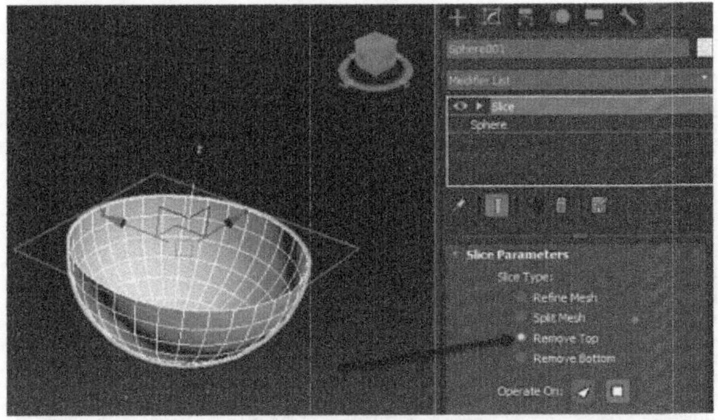

Figure 109 *Click remove tap option*

SPHERIFY

Built in 3ds Max Creation Graph # MCG. The neat thing about this spherify modifier is that, it is much more flexible than the old spherify modifier. It allows you to go beyond 100%, lock the deformation to desired axis, and it allows you to pick another object as the center of the effect.

Step 1: Create a box.

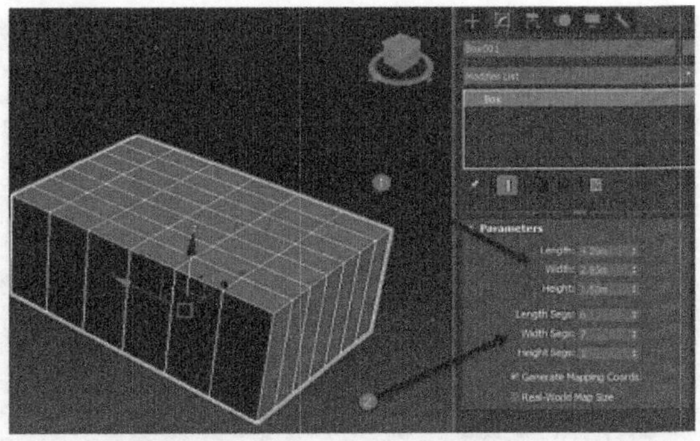

Figure 110 *Box*

Step 2: Click on modify tab and select spherify tool.

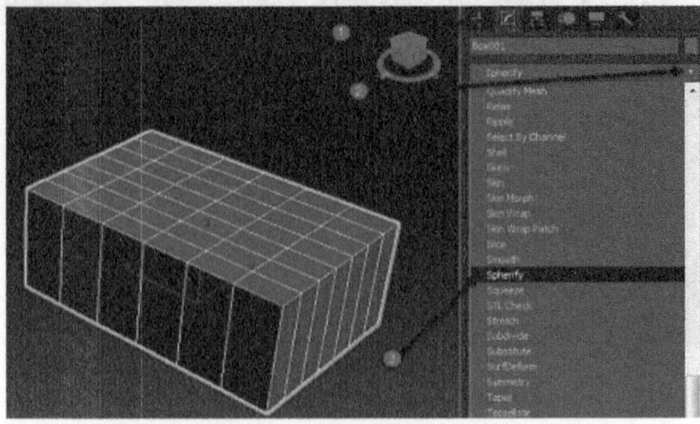

Figure 111 *Select spherify tool*

Step 3: Specify percent value.

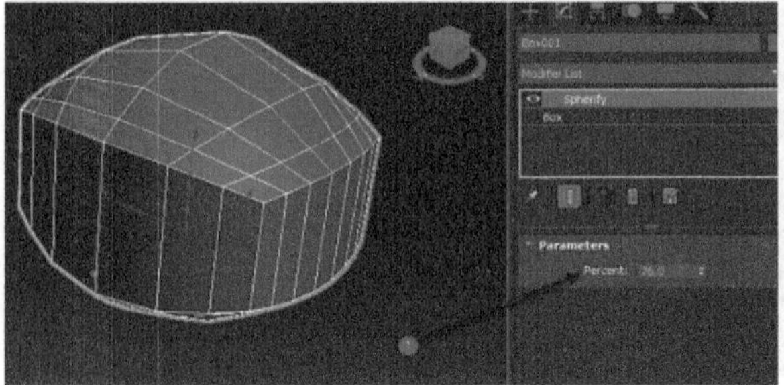

Figure 112 *Specify percent value*

SQUEEZE

The Squeeze modifier let you apply a squeezing effect to the objects, in which the vertices closest to the objects pivot point move inward. The squeeze is applied around the Squeeze gizmo's local Z-axis. You can also use Squeeze to create a bulge on the vertical axis, to accentuate the squeeze effect.

Step 1: Create a box.

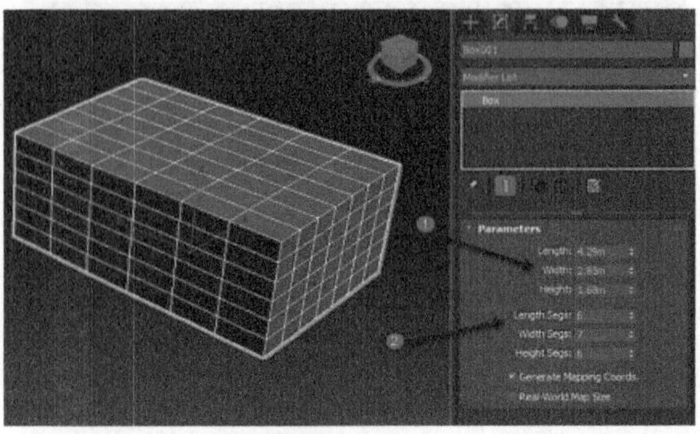

Figure 113 *Box*

Step 2: Click on modify tab and select squeeze tool.

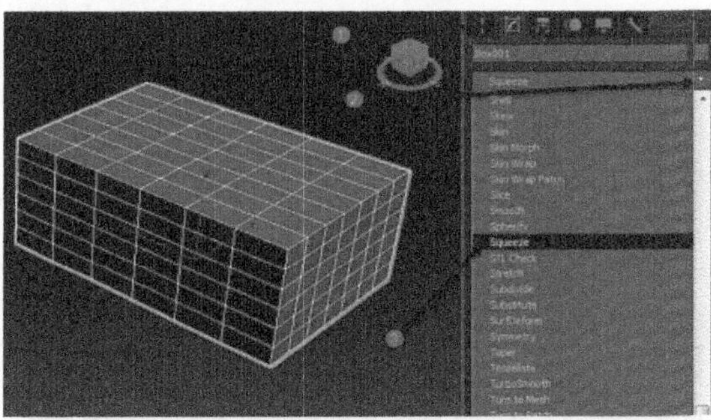

Figure 114 *Select squeeze tool*

Step 3: Set parameters as you want.

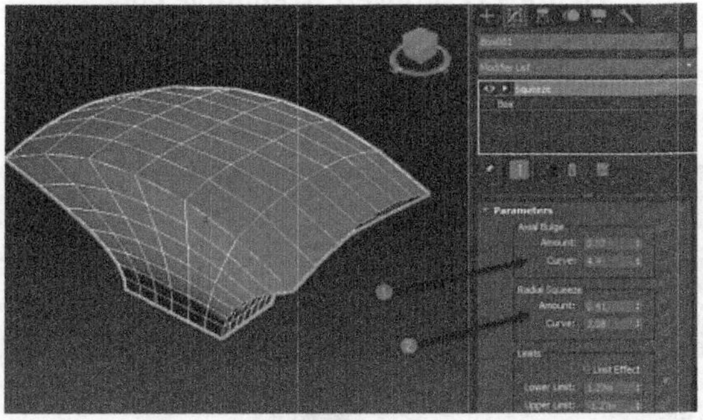

Figure 115 *Specify parameters*

STL CHECK

The STL Check modifier checks an object to see if it's correct for exporting to an stereo lithography (STL) file format. Stereo lithography files are used by the specialized machines to produce prototype physical models based on the data in the STL file.

Step 1: Create a sphere.

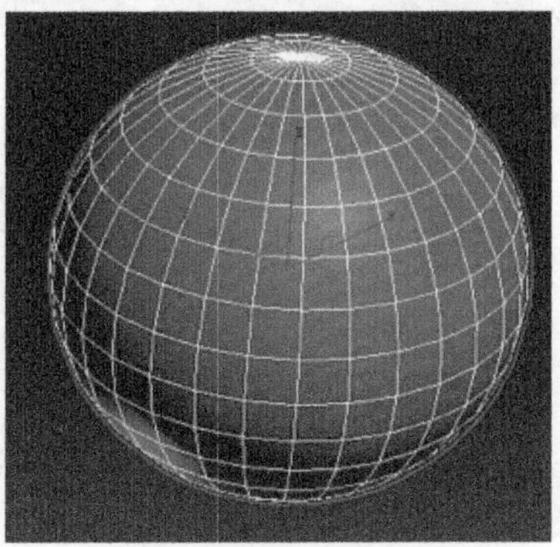

Figure 116 *Sphere*

Step 2: Convert the sphere to editable poly by right clicking on sphere.

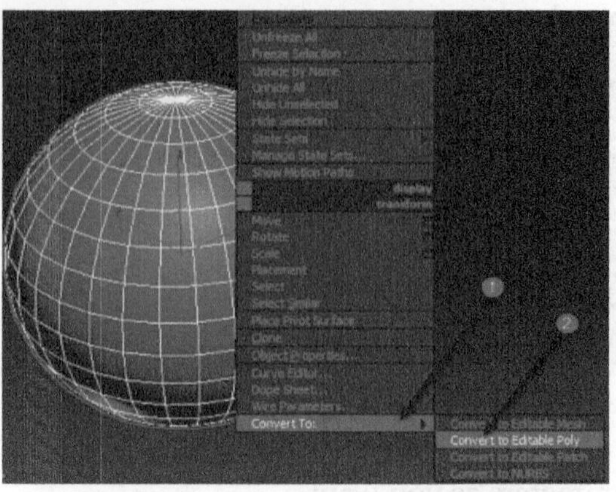

Figure 117 *Convert to editable poly*

Step 3: Click on the polygon option of Editable poly. Then select a face of Sphere and delete.

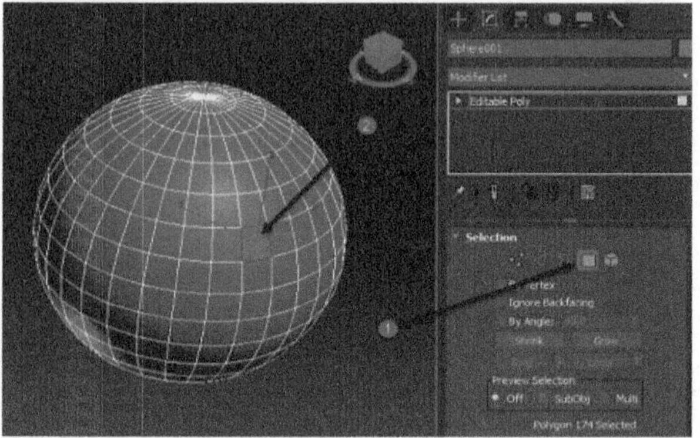

Figure 118 *Select face and delete*

Step 4: Click on the element option of Editable poly. Then select sphere.

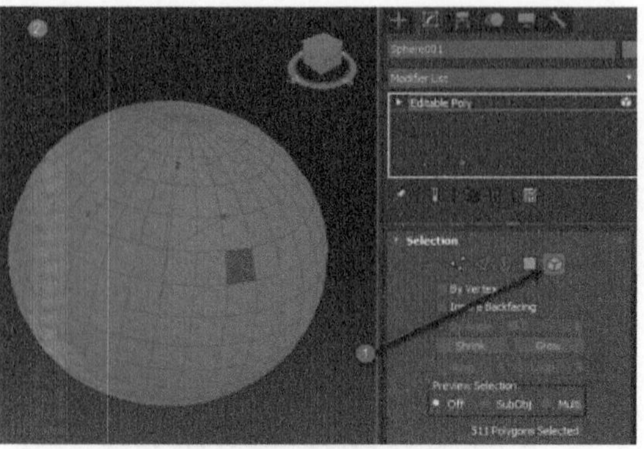

Figure 119 *Select element*

Step 5: Click on modify tab and select Stl check tool.

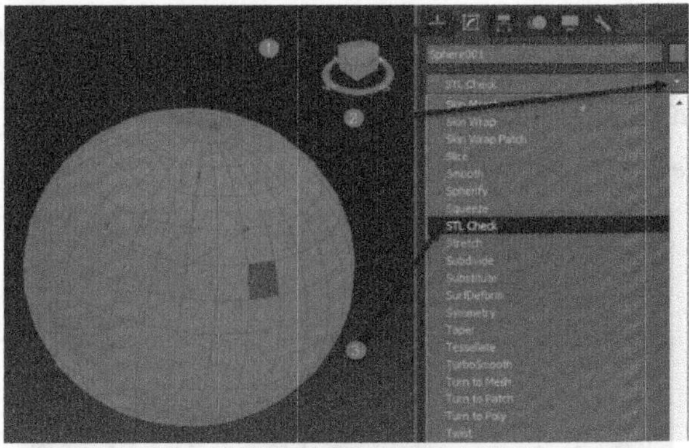

Figure 120 *Select stl check tool*

Step 6: Select everything option and tick check option.

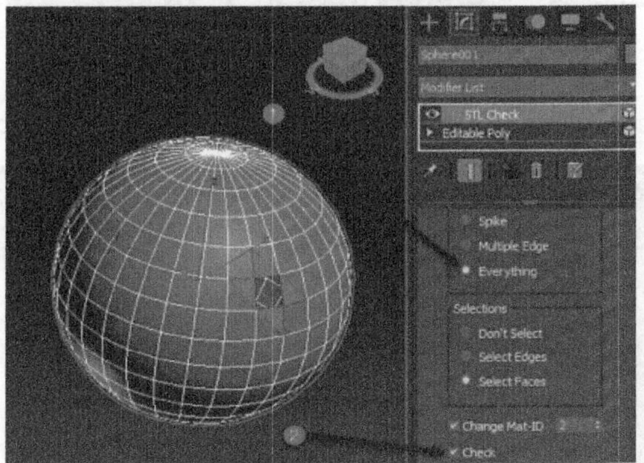

Figure 121 *Set parameters*

The error can be caught in this way. There are four errors here.

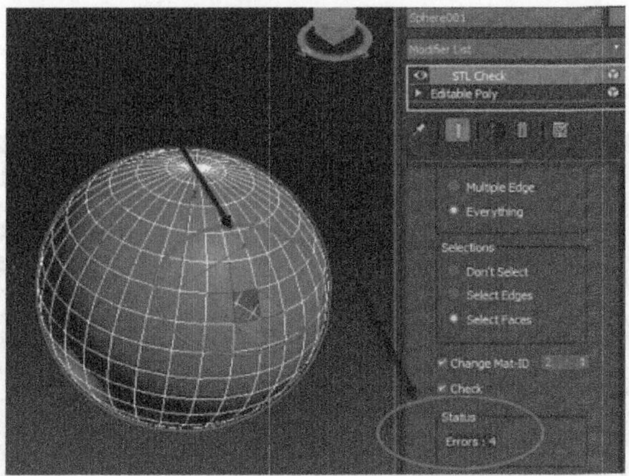

Figure 122 *Found error*

SUBSTITUTE

The Substitute modifier let you quickly replace one or more objects with another in the viewports or at render time. The substitute object can be instanced from the current scene or can be referenced from an external file.

Step 1: Create a teapot and a box.

Figure 123 *Teapot and box*

Step 2: Select box and Click on modify tab. Then select substitute tool.

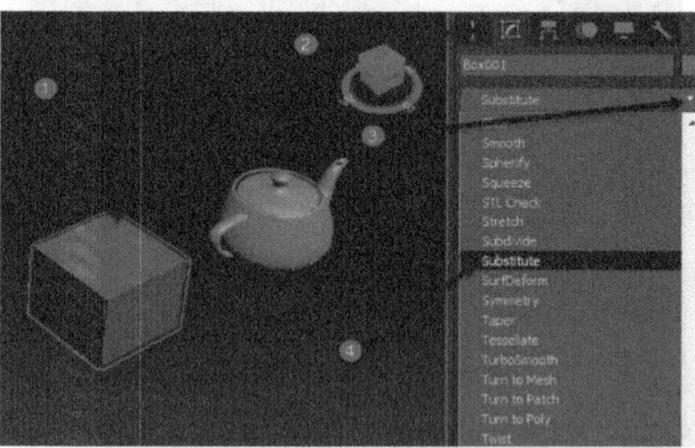

Figure 124 *Select substitute tool*

Step 3: Click on button of pick scene and pick teapot.

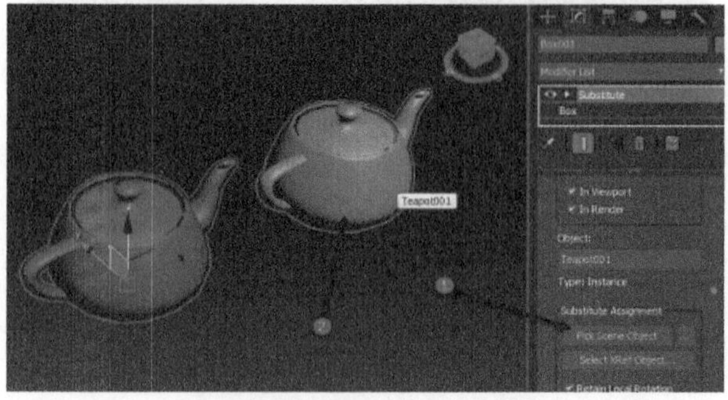

Figure 125 *Pick object*

SYMMETRY

The Symmetry modifier, not only creates a mirror image of an object for you, but also let you manipulate both sides in tandem in an intuitive way. Now, move one of the vertices on the left side of the box, where it overlaps the symmetry box.

Step 1: Create a Sphere.

Figure 126 *Sphere*

Step 2: Click on modify tab and select symmetry.

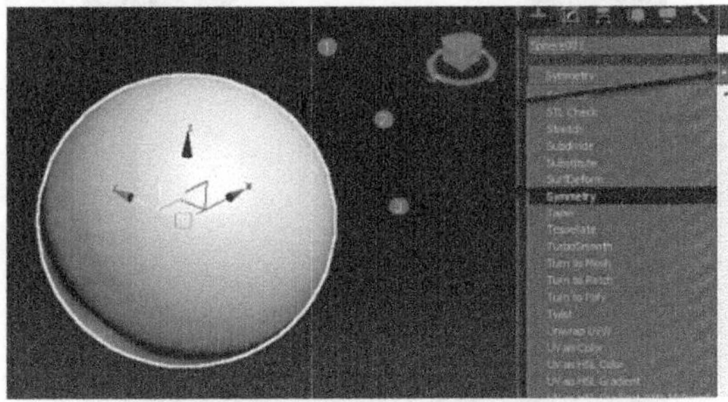

Figure 127 *Select symmetry tool*

Step 3: After that, click on flip arrow of symmetry and pick mirror option. Then select X-axis of mirror axis.

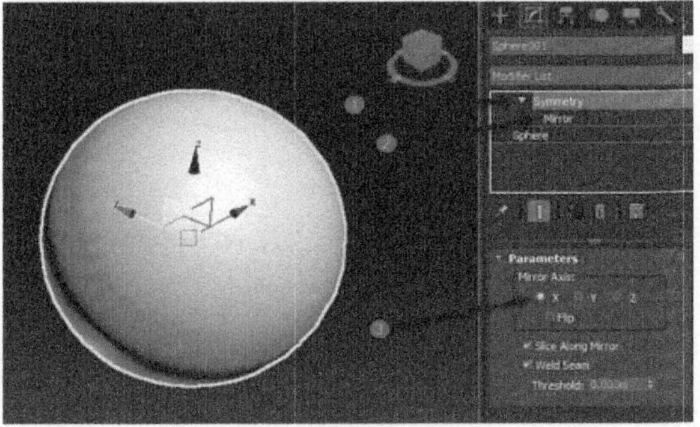

Figure 128 *Select mirror option and mirror axis*

Step 4: Click on X-axis of move icon and drag.

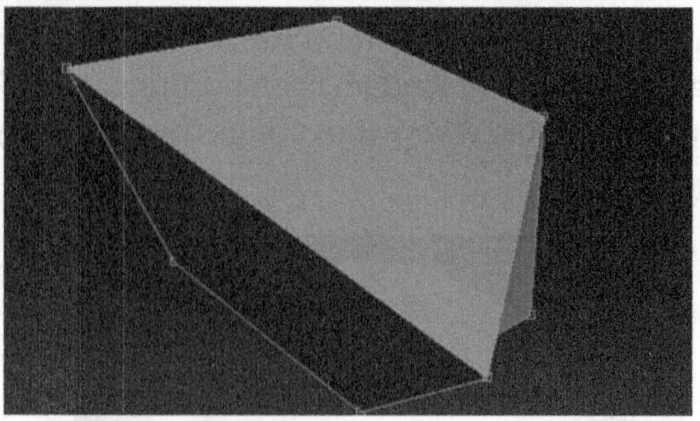

Figure 129 *Drag x axis*

TAPER

The Taper modifier produces a tapered contour by scaling both ends of an object's geometry; one end is scaled up, and the other is scaled down. You can control the amount and curve of the taper on two sets of axes. You can also limit the taper to a section of the geometry.

Step 1: Create a sphere.

Figure 130 *Sphere*

Step 2: Click on modify tab and select taper.

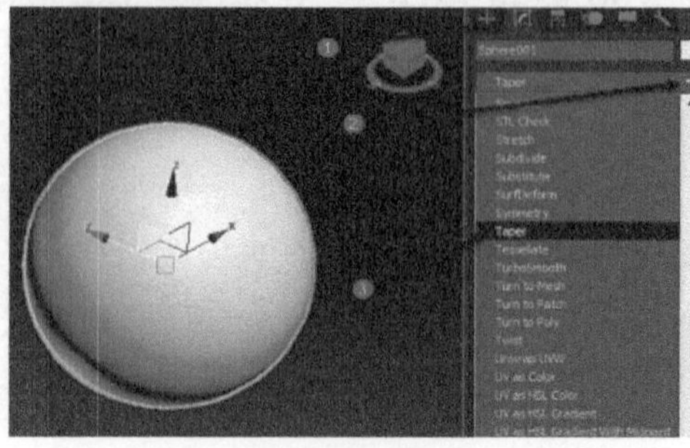

Figure 131 *Select taper tool*

Step 3: Specify taper axis and amount.

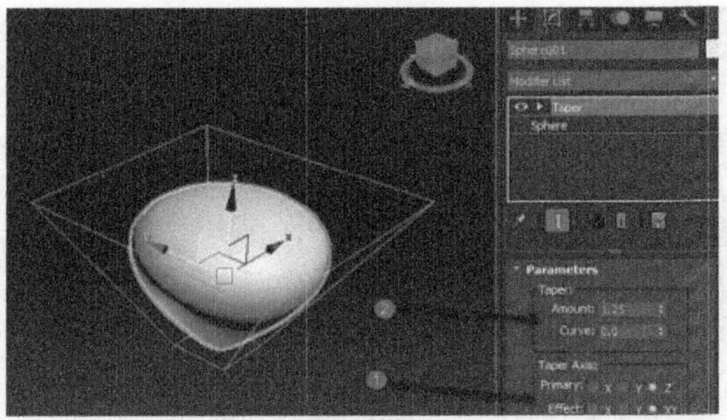

Figure 132 *Specify parameters*

TESSELLATE

By subdividing the object with the tessellate tool, you can operate in your own way. So it provides extra smoothness on curved surfaces for renderings.

Step 1: Create a box.

Figure 133 *Box*

Step 2: Convert box to editable mesh. So, right click on an object.

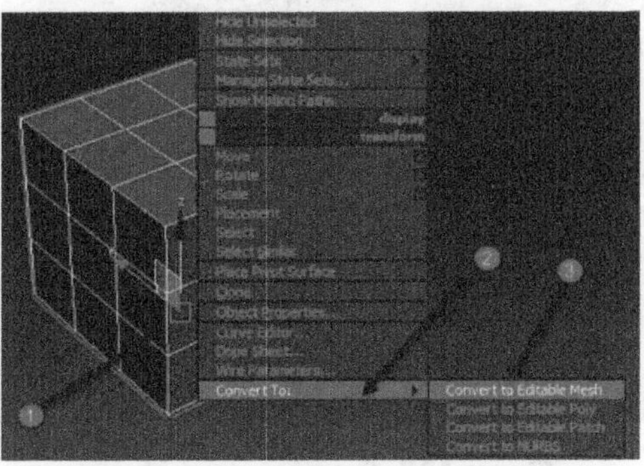

Figure 134 *Convert to editable poly*

Step 3: Click on polygon option and select a face.

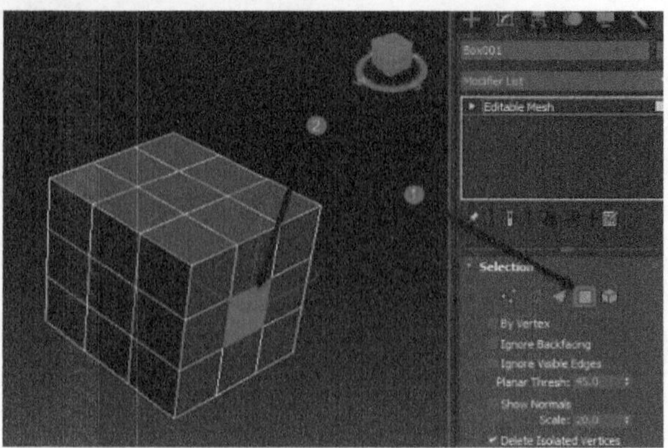

Figure 135 *Select face*

Step 4: After that, click on modify tab and select Tessellate tool.

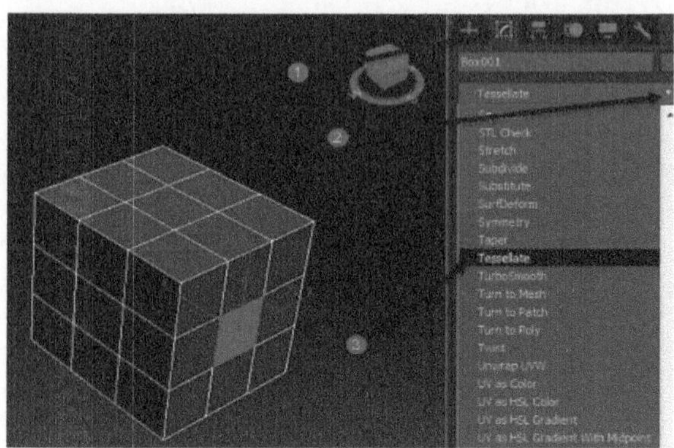

Figure 136 *Select Tessellate tool*

Step 5: Specify parameters then click on update button.

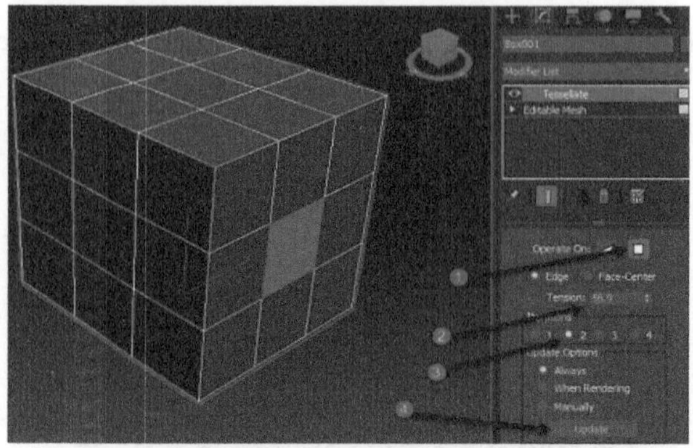

Figure 137 *Specify parameters*

TURBOSMOOTH

When off, 3ds Max displays all faces added by TurboSmooth; thus, higher Iterations values result in a greater number of lines. Let's the TurboSmooth modifier compute normals for its output, which is faster than the standard method 3ds Max uses to compute normals from the mesh object's smoothing groups.

Step 1: Create a box.

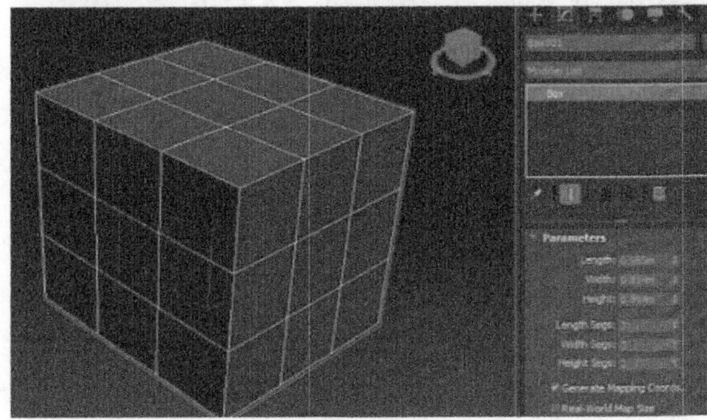

Figure 138 *Box*

Step 2: Click on modify tab and select turbosmooth tool.

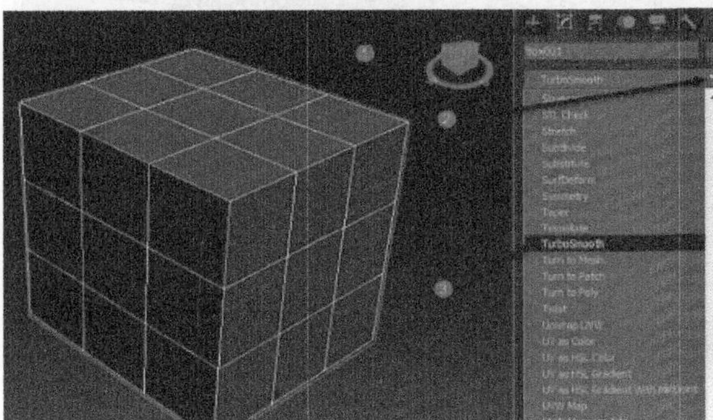

Figure 139 *Select turbosmooth tool*

Step 3: Specify iterations value.

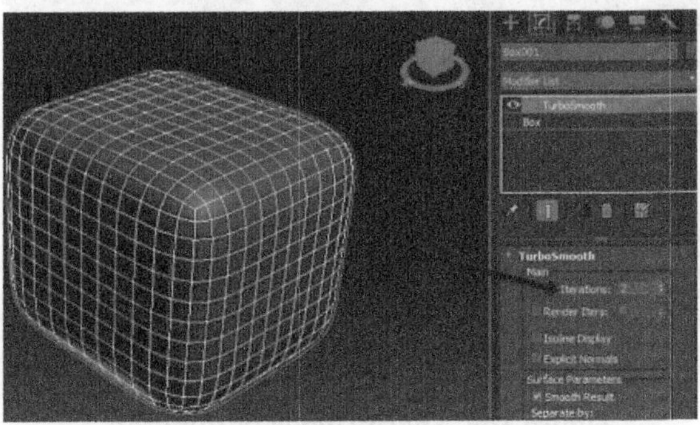

Figure 140 *Specify parameters*

WAVE

Wave uses a standard gizmo and center, which you can transform to increase the possible wave effects. The Wave space warp has similar features, and is useful for applying effects to a large number of objects. An object with the Wave modifier applied. Amplitude 1 and 2 can be changed, creating different profiles.

Step 1: Create a plane.

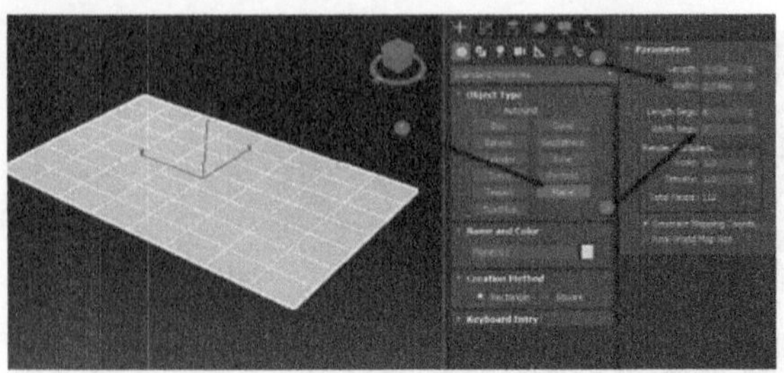

Figure 141 *Plane*

Step 2: Click on modify tab and select wave tool.

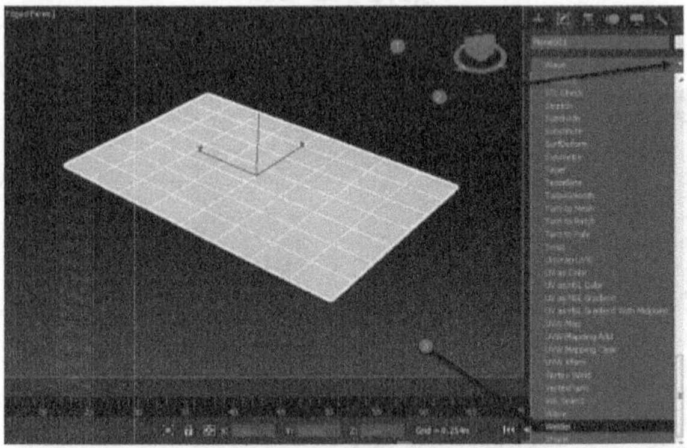

Figure 142 *Select wave tool*

Step 3: Specify wave parameters.

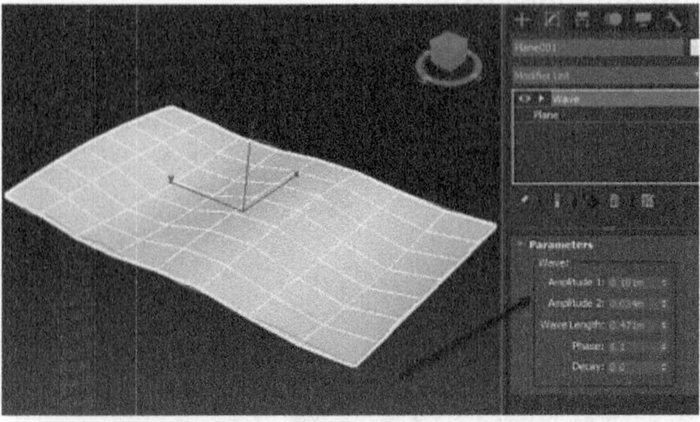

Figure 143 *Specify wave parameters*

CHAPTER-5

Basic Tools

MOVE

Use move tool to move object from one position to another. Multiplex copy of any object can also be done with move tool. But also use Shift button with the move tool to copy.

Step 1: Click on move tool.

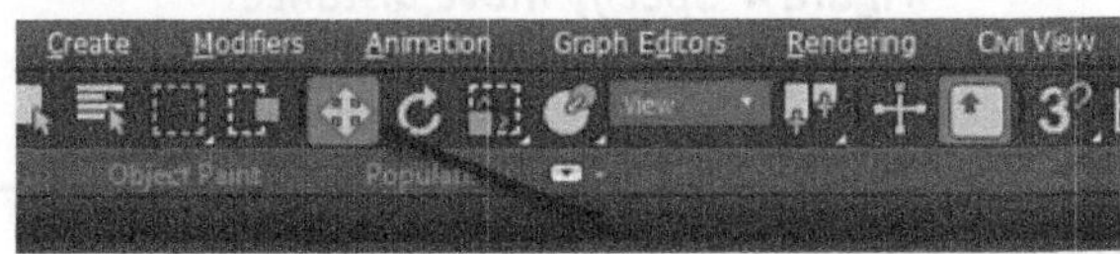

Figure 1 *Select move tool*

Step 2: Select object and drag X-axis.

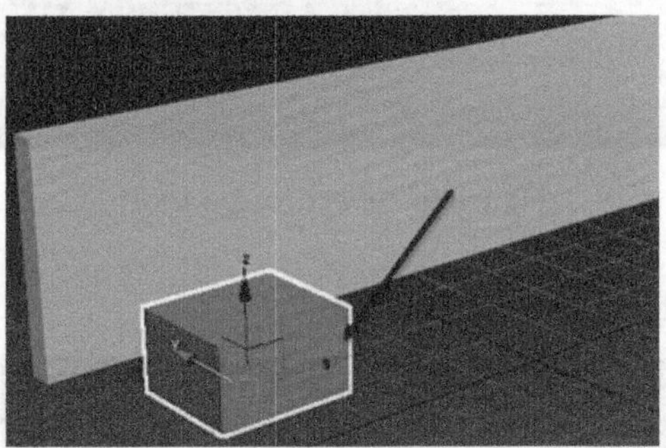

Figure 2 *Drag x axis*

OR

Step 1: Right click on the move tool.

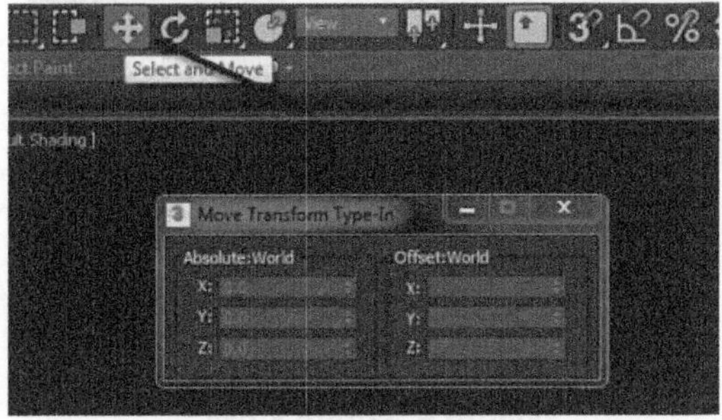

Figure 3 *Move transform*

Step 2: Select object and specify X value. Then enter.

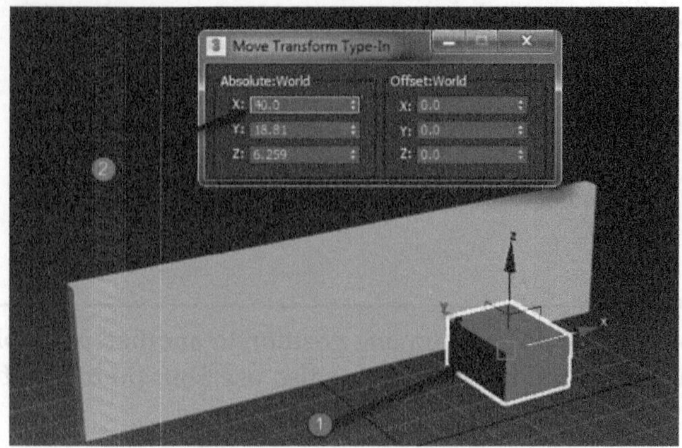

Figure 4 *Specify move distance*

ROTATE

Rotate tool is used to rotate the object around any axis.

Step 1: Click on rotate tool.

Figure 5 *Select rotate tool*

Step 2: Select object and rotate Y-axis.

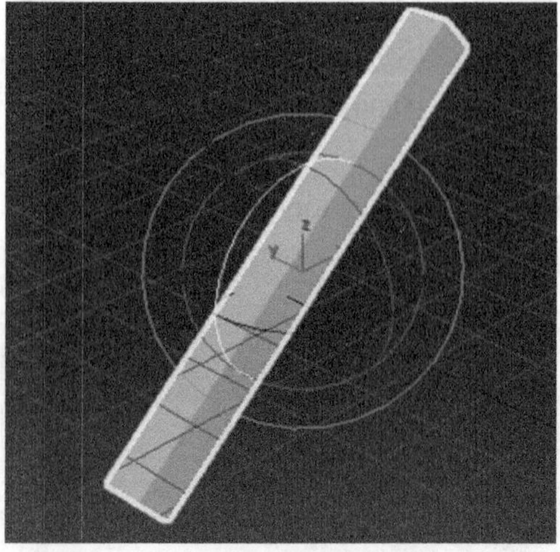

Figure 6 *Rotate Y-axis*

OR

Step 1: Right click on the rotate tool.

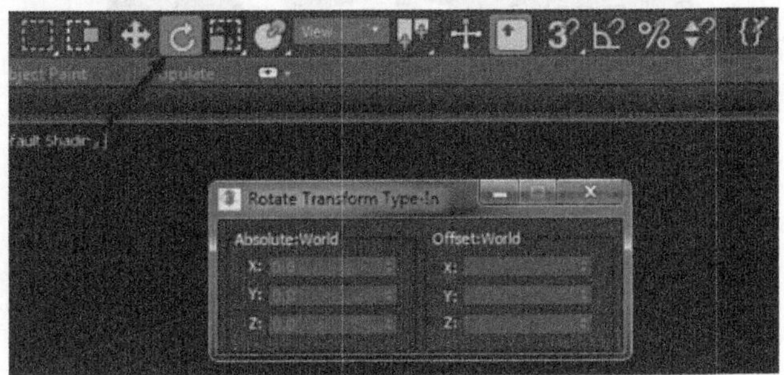

Figure 7 *Click rotate tool*

Step 2: Select object and specify Y-axis value. Then enter.

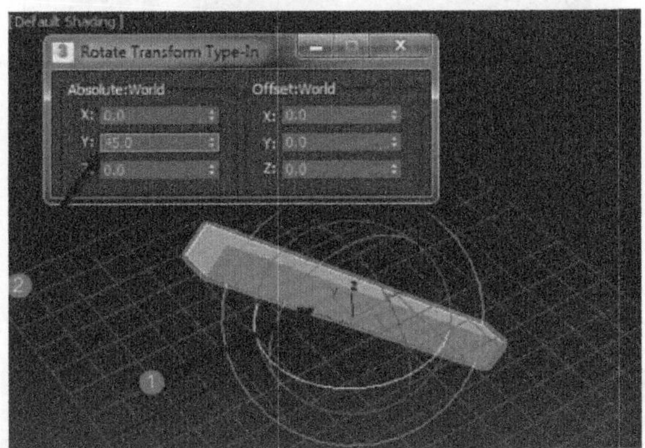

Figure 8 *Specify Y-axis value*

SCALE

Scale tool is used to increase or decrease the size of any object. Scale tool can scale multiple size.

Step 1: Click on the scale tool.

Figure 9 *Scale tool*

Step 2: Select object then click on scale tool and drag.

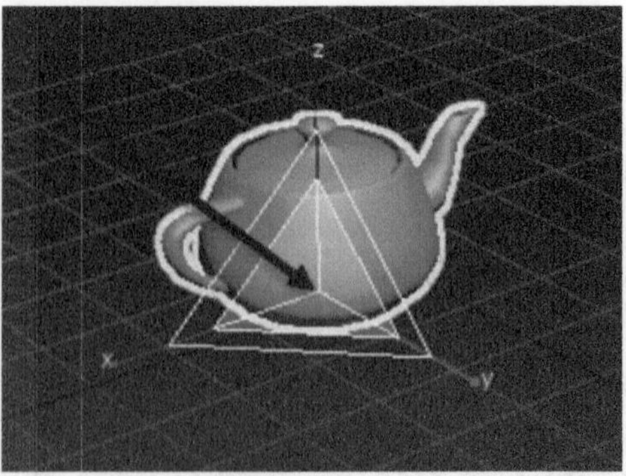

Figure 10 *Drag scale icon*

OR

Step 1: Right click on the scale tool.

Figure 11 *Scale tool*

Step 2: Select object, then specify x, y, and z value.

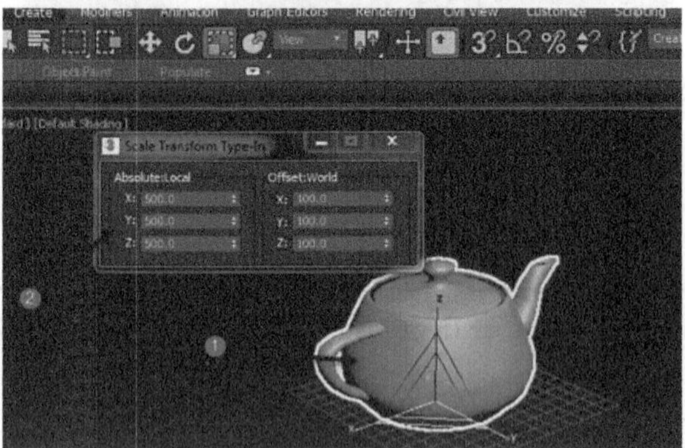

Figure 12 *Specify scale value*

MIRROR

Use mirror tools to create a mirror of any object. The mirror can also be done about axis.

Step 1: select object then click on mirror tool.

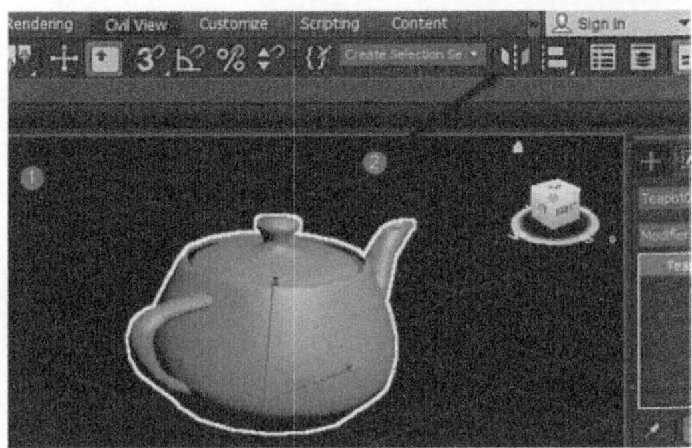

Figure 13 *Teapot for mirror*

Step 2: Set parameters like mirror axis, offset distance.

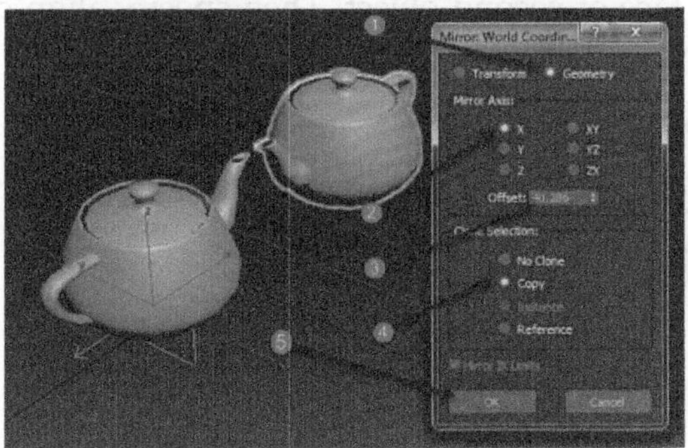

Figure 14 *Set parameters*

ALIGN

Align tool has different types. But the use of the normal ally tool does much more. It joins two objects attached to both different faces.

Step 1: Select object, then press to align tool and select normal align tool.

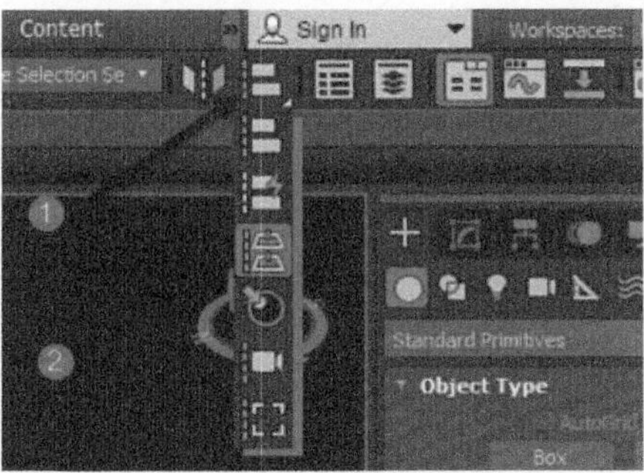

Figure 15 *Align tool*

Step 2: Select face of first object for align.

Figure 16 *Select face for align*

Step 3: Select face of second object. Then specify align distance if you want, otherwise click on OK.

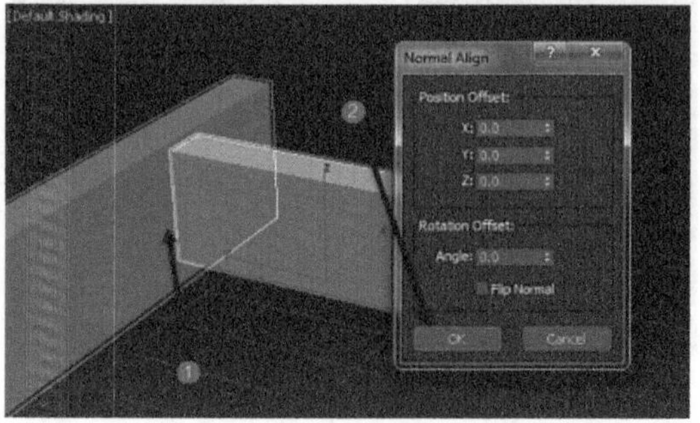

Figure 17 *Select another face for align*

CHAPTER-6

Advance Modeling Tools

LIGHTS

Use Light to give an effect to the model. By applying light, the image looks much better. Such as shining, there is a different type of light on here. That's something like the following:

1. **Photometric**
   Command panel: Create ➡ Light ➡ Photometric
2. **Standard**
   Command panel: Create ➡ Light ➡ Standard
3. **Arnold**
   Command panel: Create ➡ Light ➡ Standard

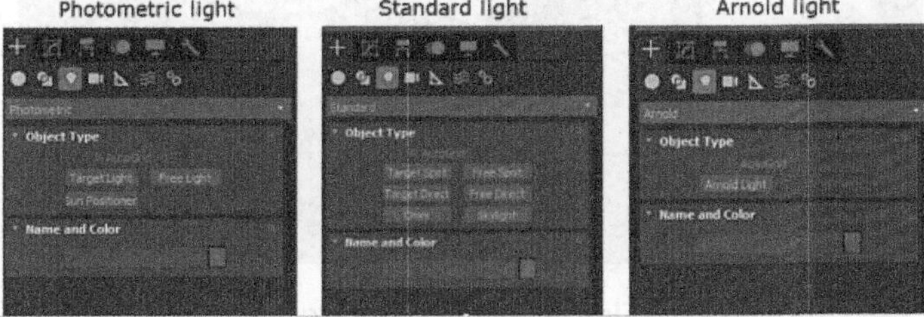

Figure 1 *Light type*

LIGHT EFFECT

Figure 2 *After lighting*

CAMERAS

The camera works in a single view. Camera help can be seen both inside and outside the model.

1. **Standard**
   Command panel: Create ➡ Cameras ➡ Standard
2. **Arnold**
   Command panel: Create ➡ Cameras ➡ Arnold

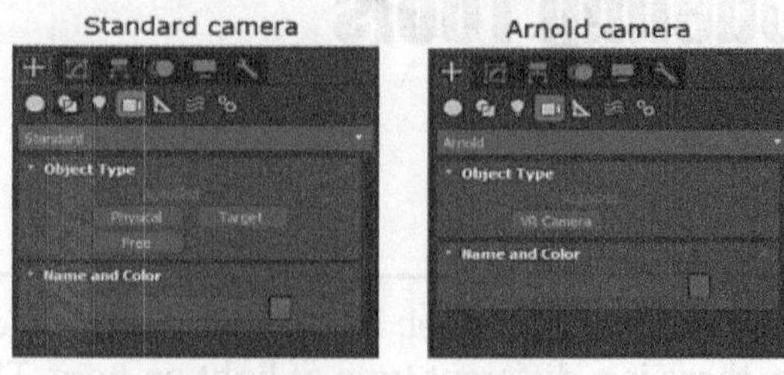

Figure 3 *Camera type*

Step 1: Click on free camera tool and set camera position.

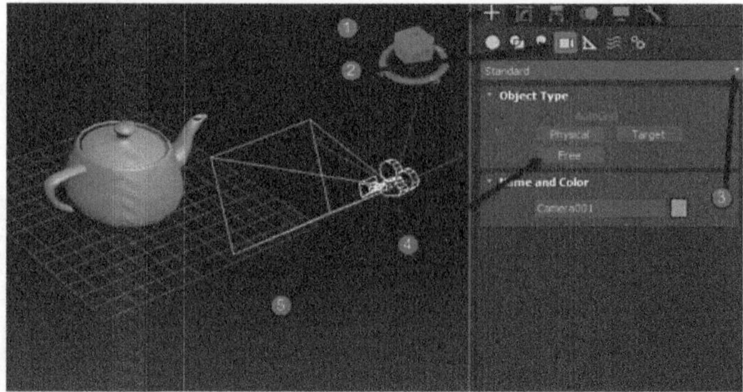

Figure 4 *Place camera*

Step 2: After that, Press C button for camera view.

Figure 5 *Camera view*

MATERIAL

Use the material to apply the material to any object such as glass, steel, or wood. The objects appear in Real view when rendering. The object can also take an image with this tool.

Material tools can be used in two ways:

1. **Tool Menu:** Rendering ➡ Material editor ➡ Slate material editor.

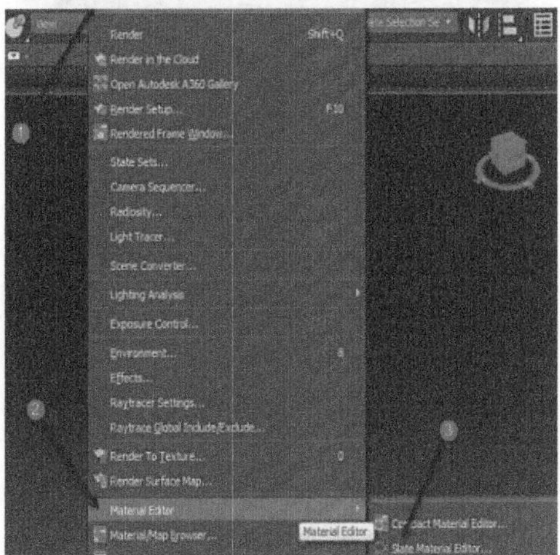

Figure 6 *Material option*

2. **Main toolbar** ➡ Material editor.

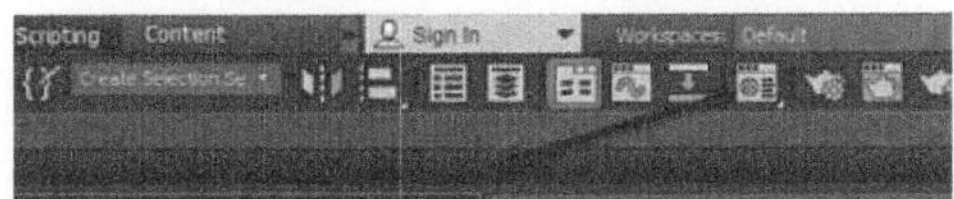

Figure 7 *Material icon*

3. Click on Material/Map browser button.

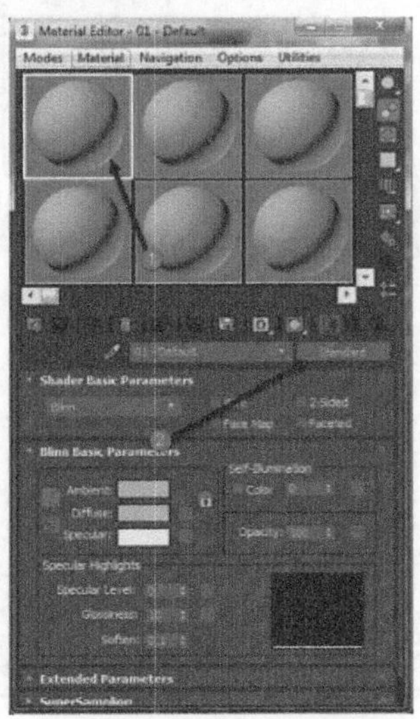

Figure 8 *Material option*

4. Select material type like Architectural.

Illegal for sale
or distribution outside
Indian Sub-continent.
Books found outside this
market may be treated as
illegal/ pirated books.

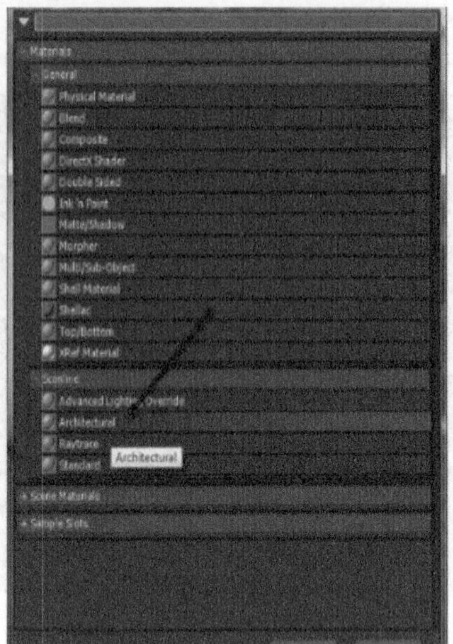

Figure 9 *Material type*

5. Click on diffuse map button.

Figure 10 *Map button*

6. Click on **Bitmap** and click on **OK**.

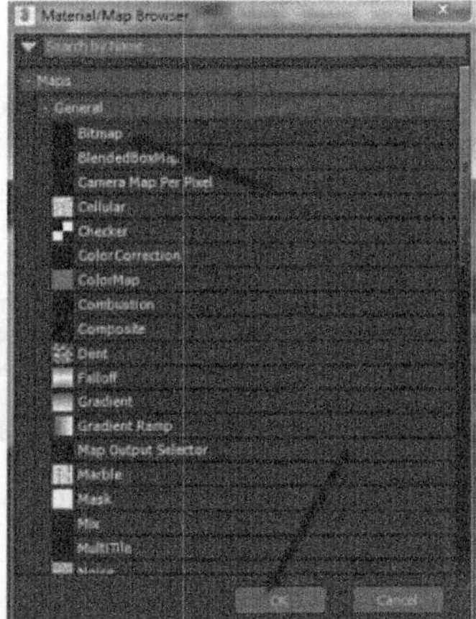

Figure 11 *Bitmap*

7. Select any image which you want and click on open button.

Figure 12 *Select image*

8. Drag material and Leave on the model. And click on show button.

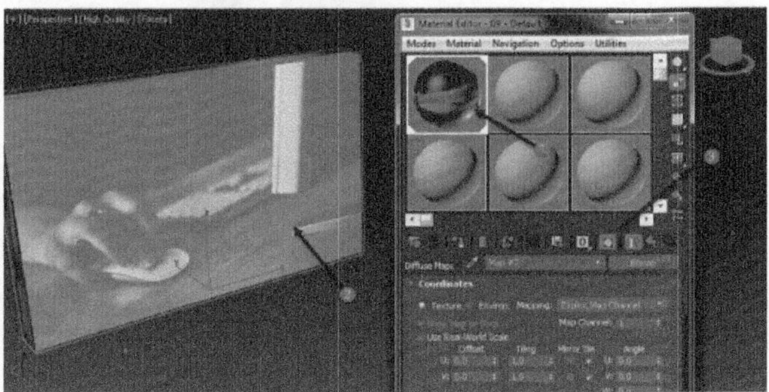

Figure 13 *Drag material*

■ Render

The render tool is used to make the photo real. Use the rendering tool to give light effects to photos.

Step 1: Click on render tool.

Figure 14 *Click render tool*

OR

Shift + Q

Step 2: Specify image size and click on render button.

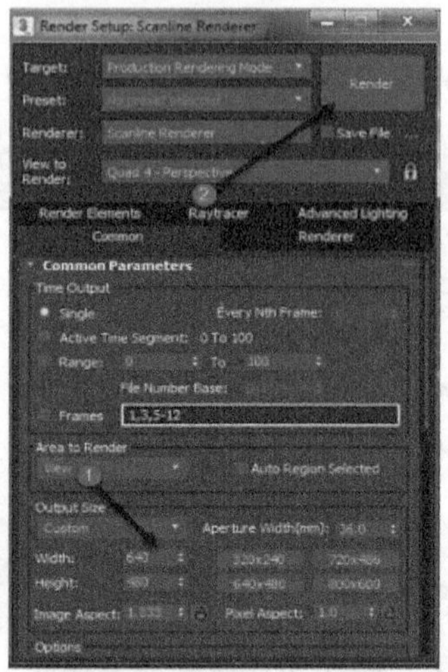

Figure 15 *Render option*

Final render image is as follows:.

Figure 16 *Render image*

■ Background image

Background setting is used to place any image in the background.

Step 1: Menu: Views → Viewport background → Configure viewport background.

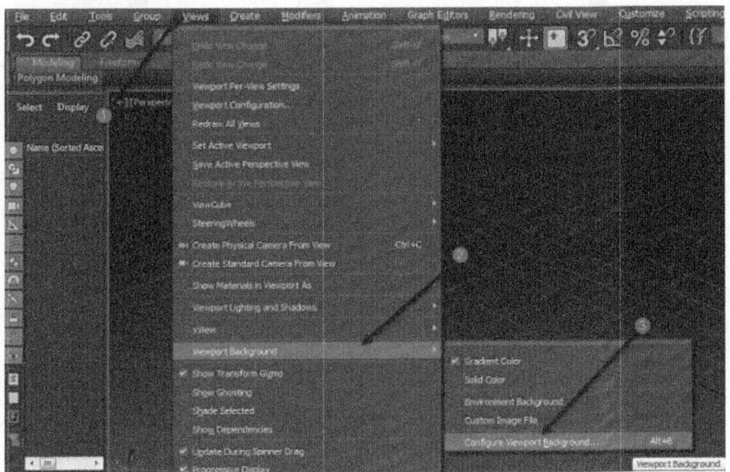

Figure 17 *Configure viewport background*

OR

Alt + B

Step 2: Click on **Use Files** radio button and click on files button.

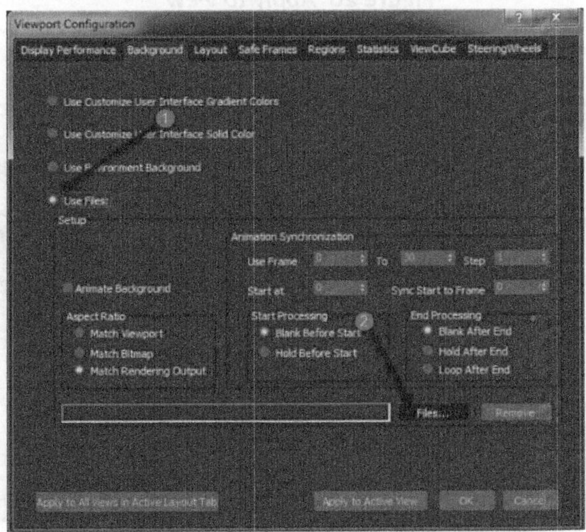

Figure 18 *Use Files radio button for browse image*

Step 3: Select the image which you want.

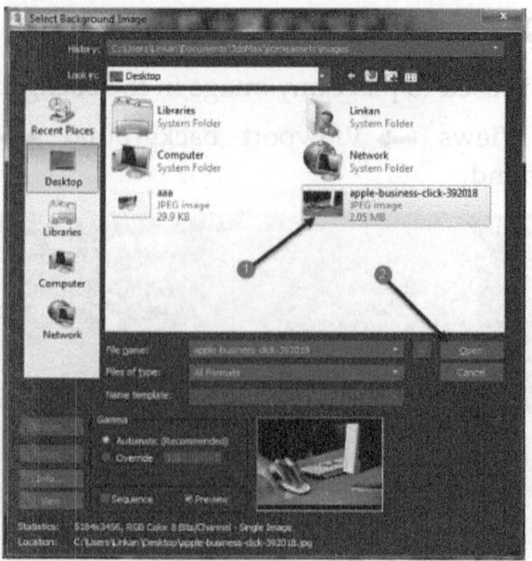

Figure 19 *Select image*

Step 4: Click on active view button.

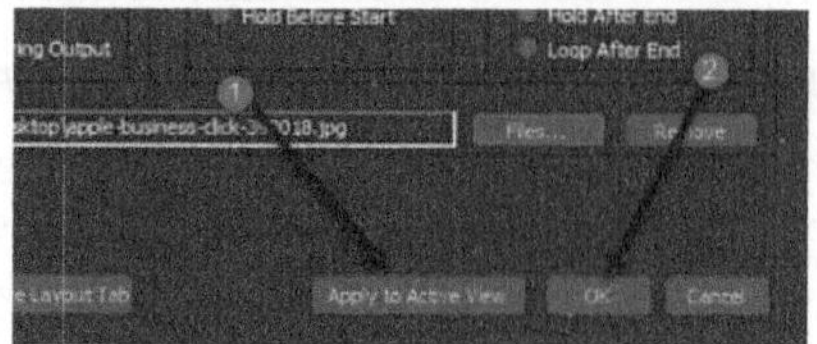

Figure 20 *Apply to view*

After that

Figure 21 *After background*